Making Property Work

An Irish Consumers' Guide

Making Property Work

An Irish Consumers' Guide

Maureen Moran

Gill & Macmillan

For Peg and Harry

Gill & Macmillan Ltd
Hume Avenue, Park West, Dublin 12
with associated companies throughout the world
www.gillmacmillan.ie
© Maureen Moran 2005
0 7171 3891 7
Index compiled by Cover To Cover
Design by Make Communication
Print origination by TypeIT, Dublin
Printed by ColourBooks Ltd, Dublin

This book is typeset in 10.5pt Linotype Minion on 13.

The paper used in this book comes from the wood pulp of
managed forests. For every tree felled, at least one tree is
planted, thereby renewing natural resources.

A CIP catalogue record for this book is available from the
British Library.

5 4 3 2 1

While every attempt has been made to ensure the accuracy of
this book, no liability can be accepted by either the author or
the publishers for the information it contains.

Contents

SECTION 2 RESIDENTIAL INVESTMENT

Acknowledgements

The author would like to thank the following people for their help and encouragement:

Seán Nyhan
Sarah Moran
Jane Moran
Finbarr Scannell
Diarmaid Ó Catháin
Deirdre Rennison Kunz
Fergal Tobin
Stephen Faughnan
Fintan McNamara
Derval Murphy

Introduction

This is a book for people who are passionate about property.

A national obsession in Ireland, property now surpasses politics as a favourite topic of conversation wherever people get together up and down the country. Irish people find it difficult to skip the property pages of a newspaper or to pass an estate agent's window without having, *'just a quick look'*, even when on holiday. We devour TV programmes on DIY and refurbishment. Do you have a fair idea of the value of every property for sale in your area? Do you ring up estate agents anonymously to enquire about places that you have no intention of buying? Do you – and this marks you out as a true addict – like to take a walk on dark evenings to get a look into other people's living rooms (not because you're nosey, but just to see how they have done them up)? You don't have to admit that one to anybody, but if you answered *'yes'* to some of these questions, and you think the time has to come to take your love affair onto a new level, then this book is for you.

Cast your eye over the shelves of any newsagent's shop and you will be amazed at just how many magazine features are devoted to house property. Editors know that property, like sex, sells. Whether it's property for sale, interior design or the chance of a peep into the houses of the rich and famous, we cannot, it seems, get enough. In the last year or two, there has been a spate of TV programmes devoted to various aspects of buying, developing and renovating homes, both at home and abroad. Their appeal lies in making the property market look easy and exciting. Some are harmless, even interesting and informative, showing us new ways to do up our homes, but many are downright dishonest. By ignoring most of the costs involved, such as professional fees and taxes, they manage to make the property market look like child's play – something it most definitely is not.

Governments have fed our addiction with a succession of policies, such as tax relief on mortgages, and a range of grants and incentives for the provision of holiday apartments, student accommodation and flats over the shops in our towns and cities. Without doubt these schemes have been useful in the right context but, on a more fundamental level, investing in your own home is by far the best way to make property work for you. This can mean buying a place to live in or extending, improving or beautifying the home you already own.

'*Affordability*' is the new buzzword in property circles with buying power replacing price as the key consideration at a time of unprecedented high prices but also low interest rates. From the high-earning professional looking for somewhere to park the laptop, to the lower income buyer trying to scrape together a deposit for a first home, people need to know how to make best use of their resources to achieve their aims in today's complex market conditions. Whether your interest lies in tax-efficient investments, local authority affordable housing or simply how to set about buying your own home, knowledge is essential to reach your goal of making property work for you. If you are buying for the first time, an old hand or an experienced landlord thinking of expanding your portfolio and trying to make sense of changes in landlord–tenant legislation, I hope you will find this book interesting and informative.

Buying your first home can be very daunting. For many it seems impossible. But every problem can be seen as a challenge. From tips on how to find that elusive 10 per cent deposit which catches many would-be buyers, to ways of making your home pay for its keep, if there is a way for you to get on the property ladder, then I feel confident that this book can point you in the right direction.

Type the word '*mortgage*' into your internet search engine and click on '*search*'. You will immediately be bombarded with advice on every conceivable type of home loan, life insurance and endowment policy. Similarly, every newspaper or magazine you pick up these days is laden with the weight of advertising for financial products. But, and this always baffles me, there is a dearth of practical information on what to look for in a property when you view it and on the nuts and bolts of buying your home or managing your investment. Where do I start? How do I know whether I am getting value for money? How do I deal effectively with the professionals: mortgage providers, solicitors and estate agents? These questions and many others will be tackled in this book as you are guided through the process, step by step, from defining your priorities and finding a suitable property to financing your project even when that seems well nigh impossible due to rising prices.

Having spent over 20 years in the property business, as a homeowner, a landlord and, for a number of years, a professional estate agent, friends and acquaintances often ask for advice and tips on buying, financing and letting property. Some, the beginners, often need only encouragement and to be told that their dreams of home ownership are not pie-in-the-sky. Once pointed in the right direction, they take off like fledglings, a little unsure at first but gaining confidence as they go. Others, older and more experienced, want to know how to manage lettings, expand their portfolios and deal with tenants. Initially, producing a handout seemed like a good idea, but I soon realised that there was just so much information to be passed on that a book was warranted.

My first encounter with the rental market was back in 1970 as a tenant in a small flat, which I shared with two other teenage girls. In those days, when all of our dreams were chaste, having a room of one's own was an unheard of luxury in most households, large families being the norm. It didn't take us long to figure out that the £15 rent we paid between us weekly, when multiplied by four (the number of flats in the building) amounted to a tidy income for the landlord. Not only that, but it wasn't higher mathematics to go from there to the realisation that we, the tenants, would have paid for the entire building between us in about seven years. Those were the good old days of high rents! Later, a stint as a Simon Community worker gave me quite a different perspective on the business of providing a roof over your head.

A chance encounter led me to become a landlord. Overhearing a woman at a meeting complain to another that she needed to sell her house quickly and was unable to get £10,000 for it, made me think. When she mentioned where she lived, I knew it was a very good letting area. I also knew I could manage to repay the £10,000 fairly easily from the rent, so the risk would be minimal. Happily, that property is still in my family. It was easy, having taken the plunge once, to repeat the process, buying properties that looked like a good bet. Over the years I have refined the operation so that now I buy only properties which offer a good return on the capital outlay.

If you harbour an ambition to become involved in the exciting, challenging and rewarding, though often frustrating, business that is letting, then Section 2 of this book will take you through the stages of finding a suitable property, calculating your likely return, organising the finance and completing the purchase. The process of advertising, finding suitable tenants and managing the letting once it is set up is also explained step by step. Landlord and tenant law is a complex area that puts many people off becoming landlords, as they fear the extent of tenants' rights. This book aims to demystify the subject, taking a common-sense look at the issues. Changes in the rights and obligations of both tenants and landlords are examined in the light of new legislation in this area.

Use this book as you see fit. In the interests of clarity I have tried to keep the first section on buying your own home as uncluttered as possible. Many of the topics touched on here are treated in greater detail in Section 2. While I have done my best to be accurate, I have no particular expertise in law, finance or building construction. The information in this book is based on my own experiences and those of my friends and colleagues in the property business. It is not meant, in any way, to be a substitute for the professional expertise of solicitors, engineers, tax advisors or estate agents. Knowing when you are equipped to handle something yourself and when you need expert help is, perhaps, the beginning of wisdom.

Success breeds success and as your confidence grows so too will the sureness of touch required to deal with the often difficult, sometimes bizarre and regularly just plain funny situations which arise in the life of a landlord.

My years in the property business have confirmed my belief in Murphy's Law – that anything that can go wrong, will. I think I have faced almost every crisis known to landlords. Without doubt I have made many mistakes, some spectacular. I have been taken in by con men (and women) more often than I care to admit, have had my properties flooded, set on fire and, in one case, almost demolished by a tiny woman driving a Fiat Bambino (don't ask; that's another story). Thankfully, I survived and did reasonably well, made many good friends and learned a little too. My wish for you, if you read this book, is that, unlike me, you won't have to learn all of your lessons the hard way. With a little knowledge and skill, you will be in a better position to avoid the pitfalls and the frustration of finding everything out *after* you've made the mistakes. If your interest in property is primarily as an investment, then I hope I can pass on some tips which will help you make a good income. May it be your road to riches beyond your wildest imagination, may you treat those who cross your path with kindness and compassion and may you have loads of fun on the way.

Section One
Your Own Home

Chapter 1
Buying Your Own Home

Seven out of ten Irish people own their own home. That's more than in most other European countries. In Germany, for example, though wages have generally been higher than here, the figure is four in ten. There are, without doubt, historical, social and cultural reasons why this is so. Since the days of the tenant farmer, the Irish have worked hard and often made great sacrifices to own their holdings whether they are houses or farms.

In modern Ireland buying a home of your own is now a major life event, taking on the significance of a rite of passage for the young (or youngish!). It is a signal to society at large that this person has become a fully fledged adult, ready to take on all the responsibilities that property ownership entails. It shows in the huge number of people eager to get a foothold on the property ladder.

According to Davy Stockbrokers, growth in the first-time buyer sector of the market has stood at an average of 16,000 annually for the past six years. Demographic trends suggest a continued increase in demand for at least the next 10 years as the rise in growth of the key 25–44 age group is predicted to continue until 2011, dip a little, and continue to grow further after 2016. As Ireland has one of the lowest ratios of households per head of population in the developed world, there is every reason to assume continued growth in this sector of the market. To satisfy demand, over 60,000 new housing units were built in Ireland in 2003 and although this figure represents a great achievement, up from 22,000 in 1993, the consensus among experts is that it is still too low.

Despite the confident predictions of the commentators who have been forecasting a drop, or even collapse, in house prices for years, prices continue to rise, if at a slower pace. By the end of 2003 the average mortgage given by the major lenders was in the region of €155,000–€170,000. At the end of 2004, that figure was €190,000. Such rapid growth in lending might be a cause for alarm were it not for significant decreases in interest rates and income tax which have made mortgages much more manageable for most purchasers.

WHY YOU SHOULD BUY

Apart from satisfying the urge many feel to build a nest, there are sound, financial reasons for investing in your own home. In addition to the benefit your investment brings in terms of comfort, status and the security of your own front door, you have the knowledge that you have a valuable asset which increases in value as you enjoy it – would that more things in life were like that!

There are two main reasons why buying rather than renting your home is such a good idea in financial terms. One is that it is relatively easy and cheap to raise the money for your purchase with a mortgage. Mortgages have, I know, had a bad press, being characterised as possessing all the charm of an albatross, but think for a moment. Just suppose somebody offered, for a small charge, to give you money that you could use to buy as asset which, on past performance, would increase in value by an average rate of about 7 per cent each year and which also had the possibility to increase by a large multiple of that amount. As an added bonus, when you wanted to sell your asset, you could do so without paying any tax on your gains. How would you react to such an offer? Personally, I'd ask if there was a catch, especially when I discovered that as part of the deal I could have free accommodation indefinitely. But this is precisely what you get when you take out a mortgage to buy your own home.

If you need other reasons to buy your first home as soon as you possibly can, then just consider the alternatives. You might, if your income is extremely low, consider relying on your local authority to house you. This sounds like a good idea until you realise that councils have never come even remotely close to satisfying the demand for houses from genuine, qualified, applicants. Waiting times of 10 years or more are not uncommon. You might consider taking your chances with the private rental sector – at least you will get a roof over your head now, and you would probably be surprised at some of the many people who have been renting successfully for years. Though often the ideal solution for those who need to be mobile, renting can have its drawbacks as a permanent answer to accommodation needs. Many people want to put down roots and put their individual stamp on their homes. New legislation improves the lot of the long-term renter as after six months you will be entitled to a four-year lease. You can still, however, be asked to vacate the property should the owner wish to sell or have a member of his own family occupy it.

Many people are unable or unwilling, for any number of reasons, to buy a home. Apart from those whose jobs require them to be mobile, there are many whose plans take them in a totally different direction, such as world travel. Possibly the idea of settling down fills them with dread. Some are the owners of businesses who put all of their money back into their enterprises.

If you belong to any of these groups long-term renting may be your best option. If we in Ireland follow the trends set in other European countries we should soon see far greater numbers who continue to rent throughout their lifetime. There are others who wish to buy but who cannot come up with the necessary 10 per cent deposit or cannot get a mortgage because their jobs are not permanent. Later in this book you will find some suggestions on overcoming many of the obstacles to home ownership. For those already at the starting blocks let's have a look at some options.

WHAT YOU SHOULD BUY

Do I want a house or an apartment? City centre, suburbs or a rural location? How much can I spend? These are some of the initial questions you have to ask yourself. You can save yourself a huge amount of frustration and wasted time by being clear in your mind about what you want from your home right from the start. If you are a first-time buyer the overriding factor determining your choice of property is likely to be price, but even within severe financial con-straints there are always some choices available. While not wishing to minimise or deny anybody's difficulties, sometimes what is needed is to see a broader picture, to think outside the conventional way of looking at things. An idyllic rural cottage could be in the same price range, or much cheaper, than a city apartment. Does this fact make you think? Study the property pages of the papers in the area in which you want to live. If you have access to the internet see what's available there. Browsing will focus your mind and give you a feel for what you want and the price you can expect to pay for it. Don't be alarmed or overly discouraged by the prices. It seems daunting to everybody at first. We have all had to start somewhere and while prices were much lower a decade ago, interest rates were sky high, almost up to a staggering 20 per cent per annum at one point. Much of the current coverage of the property market in the media is sensationalist and negative. Good news, they say, never sells newspapers. The prevailing wisdom would have us believe that it is impossible for young people to buy their own homes. I don't accept this in most cases. *'Where there's a will there's a way'* so don't be easily defeated. Make owning your own home a priority and while it might take a while to make your dreams a reality, if you keep your goal firmly in view you will at least be going in the right direction.

A few questions should help you prioritise your needs. Take your time to think about each of them. Question anyone you can who has been through the process of buying a home. Don't be afraid to ask their advice. This is a time to listen and to learn from others.

What Sort of Lifestyle Do You Have?
If your preference is for restaurants and nightclubs ditch any romantic ideas you have about a country cottage. How will you make the journey home from the pub after a few drinks? If, on the other hand, you would like nothing more than to breed large dogs and read books by the fire in the evenings, then a country retreat might be just what you are looking for. This might seem very obvious, but you would be amazed how many people think they can, quite easily, change the habits of a lifetime if they make a geographical shift. They try to buy a lifestyle rather than a building. Look at the realities of your current life and find a place to accommodate them – not the other way round. The only exception to this rule is if, having done your research and considered all of the possibilities outlined in this book you still find owning a home of your own unattainable, then you have to consider another location and perhaps a major shift. Spread your net wide and think about the employment possibilities in other areas. If you cannot afford a house, perhaps you could buy a site as one couple I know did.

They lived in a caravan on their site until they could get a mortgage – not ideal, but not bad either. In the meantime they carried on with the background work, getting plans drawn up, getting planning permission, getting quotations from builders, and so on. In the process they learned a great deal and were ready to start building as soon as they had taken care of all the red tape.

Are You Interested In Doing a Place Up?

If you are working full-time you need to think carefully before committing yourself to a place needing a lot of work. A friend I know made restoring an old house her life's work and loved every minute of the experience, but it took all of her money and most of her free time for 20 years! In addition, she reared her family into adulthood on a building site. By the time the place was finished her children were just about ready to fly the nest, so painstakingly and beautifully restored. On the other hand, this may be your best option for other reasons. If so then the advantage is that, once a place is habitable, renovations can continue, as money becomes available. Go for a smaller property rather than a large pile, especially if you are a beginner. An electrician I know, working in a very rundown house seven or eight years ago, was offered the place for sale for £20,000. He immediately accepted the offer and made a flat for himself on the ground floor. Without even doing the place up any further he sold it recently for almost €300,000. Not everybody can expect to be this lucky.

What Features Are 'Must Haves' for You?

For me it's a garden. It's not that I'm an avid gardener, but I couldn't bear not to be able to walk into the fresh air from my kitchen on a warm summer's day. I also like to have a place to read and write; this means a space with a large table or desk where there is good lighting. What are your interests? How many bedrooms do you need? Don't forget to project a little into the future here. Your needs might change. If you have small children you may need a play area in or close to the kitchen. With teenagers you need different rooms where they can do their own thing rather than larger, open-plan areas. What about bathrooms? Are you happy enough with one or do you think you cannot imagine living without two, or even three. Do you like to entertain? If so, do you need a formal dining room or would you prefer a large kitchen which could accommodate a dining area? All these things have to be considered, so really think about what is important to you.

How Important to You is Your Car?
If you possess a top-if-the-range BMW you will probably need secure parking, or maybe even a garage. If, like me, you see your old jalopy only as a means of getting from A to B, then all you need is access to street parking.

Do You Like to Be Trendy?
If you do, and you can afford it, why not? There are new urban options like converted warehouses and city-centre apartments. In the country you could go for stone-built farmhouses, ideally with a sea-view and preferably in or near a fashionable town or village. Be warned, however, trendy properties never come cheap and trends change. The exception to this rule comes in the shape of tax incentives offered to both owner-occupiers and investors in certain urban and rural locations targeted for renewal. These schemes are well worth considering, but do not expect to get such a property in a prosperous, leafy suburb. See Chapter 3 for more details.

How Close to Your Do You Need to Be?
How far are you prepared to travel each day? This is a huge issue in Dublin where people can spend up to four hours a day in the car going to and from work. I'm told people have taken up new interests like learning a foreign language, knitting and listening to books on CD to while away these hours. I've actually seen people more or less dress themselves and carry out a full skincare and make-up routine en route, so maybe a long commute is not without some advantages.

> **Remember**
> Buy a place that suits you.
> Don't try to suit yourself to the place.
> It won't work.

This is not meant to be an exhaustive list of questions, just a device to get you thinking about what you want from your home. Think carefully about your daily activities and what would make life as easy and pleasurable as possible. Look closely at the needs of your family, and at how you live and work, so that the home you buy will be right for you. Write things down as they strike you. Have a brain storming session with your family. Take your time and you will get it right. Be realistic, however. Don't expect to clear your mind overnight and don't insist that everything on your list is necessary. Compromise is essential. If you succeed in finding a property at the right price that has the most important things you want, then be grateful and go for it.

WHICH PROPERTY: NEW OR OLD?
Old Properties

I have lived in both new and old houses. For me there are few pleasures in life (not either sinful, illegal or fattening) to compare with a glowing fire on a cold winter's evening in a house where time, and all the people who have lived there, have left a positive imprint. I firmly believe that we all leave something of ourselves after us in the places where we live. How else can you explain the difference in atmosphere between otherwise similar houses? It has happened occasionally, on walking into a house, that a shiver went down my spine. Other times I've felt instant warmth and contentment in a house. My current home is over 100 years old. Before we moved in it had gone to wrack and ruin. The surveyor found just about every horror in his handbook: dry rot, wet rot, woodworm, leaky piping, dodgy electrics and crumbling windows. The funny thing was that no matter how awful the décor, how unreliable the plumbing, people who live here invariably loved it. They felt the warm, contented glow that seeps from the pores of the walls. Nobody was glad to leave this house. They left reluctantly when their time was up. Although we had the place completely refurbished before we moved in, for me the magic is still there.

All of this sounds hopelessly romantic I know. Some older properties are money pits. Make sure you have a thorough survey carried out if you are considering and older property. This will give you a good idea of how much needs to be done. Where major renovations are to be carried out, it might also be a good idea to engage a quantity surveyor who will give you an accurate assessment of the cost of the project and the likely timescale. If you engage an architect or engineer he should be able to perform this function. Be cautious and watch your costs carefully. Once begun, renovation jobs tend to take on a life of their own. Not only is it difficult to decide just how far to go, to know how much is absolutely necessary to maintain the place, and how much is merely cosmetic, but it's hard not to get carried away. A few more sockets in the living room, some unplanned halogen lights in the kitchen, better quality tiles in the bathroom and before you know it, and you're in trouble as the price of the job has doubled. Inexperienced people who do not engage in proper planning are often surprised by relative costs. They think that something large will inevitably be expensive; something small, cheap. This is a myth. Walls, for example, can be relatively inexpensive; door handles, outrageous. When it comes to finishing, in fact, the sky is the limit. This is why every detail must be planned and costed at the outset. As you progress rigid discipline is required to stick to your budget.

Finally, beware of listed buildings! The law now protects many quite ordinary buildings and protection orders can apply to the interior as well as the exterior of a building. In recent times, especially in Dublin, many homeowners only discovered that their property was listed when they sought planning permission to renovate or extend. Owners of such properties are severely restricted in regard to what work may be carried out. If allowed at all, renovations must be done to very exacting specifications and can prove very costly. Resale can also be a problem, as many would-be purchasers will shy away from such an onerous responsibility.

Remember
Beware of listed buildings!

If, after all of these dire warnings, you're feeling discouraged about the prospects of an older property, then think of the advantages. With an older property you get a special home, full of character and charm, often with unique architectural features and conveniently situated in close proximity to a town or city.

Judging by the slew of TV programmes on the theme, there has been a lot of interest lately in renovating older properties, doing them up and selling them on in the hope of making a fast buck on the property market. Most of these programmes are best viewed as fantasies however. Often thoroughly misleading, they neglect to give the true cost of their operations. Though the costs of the labour and materials may be itemised for the viewer, the hidden costs of the transactions involved are often not mentioned. The economics of renovating older properties can make perfect sense when you're looking for a special place to live. If, however, your aim is to make a quick killing then you need to check out the virtually prohibitive costs of buying and selling. Stamp duty, legal and professional fees, capital gains tax, and the cost of borrowed money involve major expenditure. I have lost track of the number of times I have heard it remarked in tones of envy that a property had been sold, after renovation, for two or three times its price when purchased a short time earlier. In reality, though it can be done, it is not as easy to make money this way as it seems because the hidden costs are so high. Small builders often take on these renovations projects and do well, sometimes tiding themselves over lean periods in the industry. They possess skills and purchasing power not available to the rest of us. For the amateur, much of the apparent profit is merely house price inflation, which would have been gained anyway, even if nothing had been done to the building. I'm not saying that renovation and resale for profit is impossible, merely urging caution. You need to know what you are at.

New Properties
It is in the Irish winter that new properties really come into their own. Since the mid-eighties there have been huge improvements in the standard of building and especially the finish in new homes. Gone, for the most part, are the days of howling gales under doors, rattling windows and damp walls. With insulated walls and roof spaces and hermetically sealed windows, new houses and apartments look gorgeous and are bright and easy to heat and clean. When you buy a newly built home you can expect a lovely, new kitchen, a modern, efficient heating system and a sparkling bathroom. New houses have good storage too with full-length fitted wardrobes and understair cupboards. No maintenance other than painting should be needed for 10 or 15 years once the builder has taken care of the snag list. On the minus side is a certain lack of character, a featureless similarity to other houses in the development. Only time and the presence of those who live there confer atmosphere and character. On a more practical

level, a lot of the basics which are taken for granted in second-hand homes: fireplaces, curtains, floor coverings, even kitchens are often not included in the price of a new property. Though they may not be to your taste, at least they are there in a second-hand home, and are better than nothing when one is starting off.

The areas around the property, roads and green spaces, are part of what you're paying for when you buy a new property. There is always a risk that they may not be finished. In the past builders quite often went bust. Having completed and sold the houses they had built, they left the surroundings, the roads and so on, unfinished. Often the householders had no option but to club together and pay to have these necessities attended to – something they could ill-afford. Thankfully, as a result of a bonding system insisted on by government, those days are now mostly gone. But new areas still need time to mature a little and look less raw. When buying a new building be sure to buy only from a registered builder who offers the usual 10-year structural guarantee, giving the purchaser insurance cover for serious defects. One of the main advantages of buying newly built property is the stamp-duty exemption. This applies to all new properties which qualify for a Floor Area Certificate and are valued under €190,500. Properties valued over €190,500 and under €381,000 benefit from a reduced rate. (See Appendix 1.)

AN APARTMENT OR A HOUSE?

Apartment living – a concept that was foreign to this country until the early nineties – has taken off. Almost every town has its quota of new, gleaming, modern apartments. It's a bit incongruous really – to see apartment blocks, which are a way of saving space in an urban environment, surrounded by fields. Not only that, but while blocks built a decade or more ago might have had 10 or 20 units, now numbers from 500 to 800 are being built at a time. Not to be outdone in the race towards gentrification, the flats that we all loved in our youth are still there – they haven't gone away you know – but are now also termed 'apartments'. A variety of buyers seem to be attracted to new, custom-built apartments: investors, first-time buyers, older couples trading down to a smaller property on retirement and those new to an area. The main attraction of apartments over houses is, unquestionably, the price; the average cost of an apartment is considerably lower than that of a house. Location is often another

Remember
In general a house is a better buy then an apartment.

reason for buyers to choose apartments, as many are very conveniently situated near city centres. Some people, who are often older, prefer them because they have had enough of gardening and trying to maintain a large family home. They want to simplify their lives and see an apartment as the easier option. Investors and others are very conscious of the maintenance factor. Houses, they reckon, have gardens, driveways, several external walls and a roof, all of which need to be looked after. On the other hand, apartments have a fund for the maintenance of common areas whereby no individual purchaser has any great responsibility outside of his or her own apartment, other than to contribute the appropriate amount of money.

Personally, I think the maintenance argument in favour of apartments is exaggerated, certainly as it relates to cost. When sizeable repairs to a house are required, such as to the roof, the homeowner can employ a builder of his own choosing to do the work, someone known and trusted, who won't rip him off. However, in an apartment, the owner is reliant on the management company or owners' committee to get the work done. Where a committee has charge of the maintenance fund it can be difficult to make decisions and to get the best price possible for repairs. This fund accrues from annual charges imposed on the owner of each apartment. It is very important to find out the amount of this service charge and who handles the management before you buy. You can, of course, expect to pay higher charges if the management is done by a professional company, but I suppose you get the service you pay for.

Case Study
Meet my cousin, Madge. Her first venture into the property market was to buy her own home, a one-bedroomed apartment in a modern block in a suburb of Dublin. With great expectations of the excitement of city life, she finally picked up the keys from her solicitor one wet Friday in

November. The weekend was spent happily enough putting it all together. Curtains, kitchenware and bed linen, all of which had been lovingly collected over many months, were installed. Those first few nights were fine. It was the weekend and, with many of the residents away, the block was half-empty. By Thursday, however, Madge was reduced to a quivering wreck, a shadow of her former self, through shock and lack of sleep. She could tolerate hearing every sound that emanated from her neighbours' TVs, at least when they were all on the same channel. The toilet noises were somewhat less pleasant in the images they conjured up, but the creaking bedsprings and the cries of passion were definitely the last straw for the young woman alone in her bed, trying to get some sleep before work in the morning.

Whether you are buying a home for the first time, trading up to something bigger or downsizing because you no longer need so much space, much thought is needed before making a decision.

LOCATION, LOCATION, LOCATION

Apart from the obvious – you don't want to buy next door to a black pudding factory, unless of course you own it – the location of your home is a very subjective matter. Many buyers, and some estate agents, have the areas with which they are familiar all neatly divided up in their minds into desirable and not-so-desirable. Don't buy into such narrow thinking. While most of us will dream of an idyllic, contented life in a *'good'* area, for most first-time buyers, and many others too, this remains a dream. And what's wrong with having something to aspire to? Remember that this book is about making property work. Let's deal with current realities first and then progress from there. We can examine first the external factors, which influence your choice of location.

Area

Subject to price and convenience, look in areas where there are people with whom you have something in common. Most people like to live in communities with like-minded people, be they young professionals, families or older, retired people. Don't look exclusively in such areas, however, because you may miss out on other opportunities. It only takes a few neighbours to make a community especially nowadays when we all live busy lives and have so little time to chat.

Bear in mind too that a good mixture of age and income groups in an area can create a far richer environment in which to live. I have a horror of ghettoes, rich or poor. If you have children, for example, a few other children in the neighbourhood can make their lives more interesting. When moving with children, don't forget to find our where the schools are and what they are like. In every urban area there are different types of school. Considerations such as size, region, location and extra-curricular activities offered may influence where you choose to look for your new home. As with neighbourhoods, a good, mixed school community is ideal.

Have a browse around the shops in likely areas. Do they sell the sort of things you like to buy? Do you feel at home in the local pubs and restaurants? Answering these and other questions will ensure that you get it right.

If money is tight look for secondary locations such as older areas in cities and towns. Often such places have an abundance of well-built houses and established facilities. Though the houses themselves may need some modernisation, they can be excellent places in which to live, convenient to everything. Often, they are ex-local authority houses that have been occupied by tradesmen. As a result they are well maintained if not modern. This is good because it means that they will be cheaper to buy and often need no more than a little cosmetic work and tender loving care.

Perhaps you are considering two or more areas in which to buy. If so, remember that a smaller property in a good area will generally offer better capital appreciation than a bigger property in a poorer area.

Transport
Good transport links are vital to how we live today. Try to live near local bus routes if in the city. A railway station should, in theory, be an advantage when considering a property but many Irish railway stations are situated in older, more rundown parts of our towns and cities. Airports are another matter. If you have never been outside this country you may not see proximity to an airport as a big advantage, but someone else will and when you come to sell your house this is a

benefit that will be reflected in the price. Throughout the country new roads have changed our ability to travel longer distances more easily. Places once remote are now accessible. This means opportunities for capital growth in property. In Dublin, properties close to Dart line have experienced growth far in excess of other areas. A similar pattern is emerging already in relation to the Luas lines.

The other thing worth bearing in mind is that other perennial problem – parking. If you don't drive and have a total aversion to sitting behind the wheel of a car, then you might think that you are lucky to be in a position to choose a property that is cheaper because it doesn't have parking. Again, this is false logic. As a car increasingly becomes the favourite way for people to travel, your property is at a serious disadvantage if it doesn't have space to park a car close by.

Remember
Smaller and cheaper in a good area is a better buy than larger and more expensive in a poorer area.

WHEN YOU HAVE AN AREA IN MIND

Before you commit yourself to a particular area it is important to get to know it well. Visiting the area on a few occasions is vital. Make sure your visits take place at different times of the day and night. Some places can show quiet respectable faces during the day yet by night become sinister and dangerous to walk through. Do the journey to work once or twice in the morning and again in the evening to discover if the area is convenient for you. Do this even if it means staying in B&B for a night or two. It will be money well spent if you come to realise that the travelling distance is impractical.

Take a trip to the planning office for the region. Check the zoning in that area and if any planning applications have been approved recently. The staff are usually very helpful so you should be able to talk to the planner at least by phone if you need to clarify anything. Make sure that there are no plans for major roads, which would impinge on the enjoyment of your home.

Another good way to find out about an area is to visit one of the pubs there and strike up a conversation with some of the locals. Most people are happy to have the opportunity to talk about where they live if somebody is thinking of moving in. (This approach might be unwise if you are a single female, so bring a friend along. You might start off on a less than ideal footing if you have to give the brush-off to some of the local Lotharios even before you move in.)

Chapter 2
Number Crunching

LOOKING FOR A LOAN

Taking out a mortgage is a major financial commitment. Getting it right is essential as it can really make the difference between security and comfort or years of worry and penny pinching. The cost of repaying €200,000 over 25 years will probably amount to between €400,000 and €450,000, a great deal of money. It is necessary to get the correct balance between the term and the repayment – the longer the term the lower the monthly payments but the loan will cost you more in the long run.

A young man I met recently is currently going through the process of buying his first home. His proudest boast was that he had succeeded in persuading (or tricking?) his mortgage lender to give him a much larger loan than his income could justify. So full of confidence was he that, when my friend murmured about putting himself under too much strain, he looked amused. Youth and optimism are, indeed wonderful things, but I shudder to think what will happen to him if interest rates rise, even by a modest amount.

Reputable lending institutions have well-established rules regarding how much they will lend. These guidelines are used to assess an applicant's ability to repay and are there for a good reason. If you work within them, with the help of a good mortgage broker, you will get the best deal possible, the one that suits your individual circumstances. Remember that a good lender, one you feel you can talk to, should be seen as a partner in your quest to achieve ownership of your own home. Experienced finance providers can't be tricked easily. It is far better to be upfront in all of your dealings, earning the respect and trust or your associates. This trust factor, incidentally, is impossible to measure, but invaluable. Earn it and it will act as a lubricant the next time you wish to do business with the same people. Lose it at your peril.

Case Study
Good fortune comes in many guises. Though none of my friends has ever, as far as I know, had a substantial win on the Lotto, many have become quietly wealthy – round-heeled and well-heeled – without any fanfare.

Margaret is a good example. A teacher all her life, she bought her house, a three-bedroomed townhouse on the outskirts of Cork City in the mid-seventies for £12,700. Her savings were sufficient for the deposit and she was able to borrow the rest from a building society, quite an achievement for a single woman back then. 'The first few years were difficult,' she remembers, 'especially so when I was faced with a doubling of interest rates within 12 months of moving in. Luxuries like holidays were out of the question that year. In fact I had to think twice before buying as much as a large jar of coffee.' Her home is now worth €260,000 and three years ago she was able to release some of its value, using it as security for a mortgage on an apartment in Spain, a very satisfactory outcome, she feels.

HOMEWORK: YOUR DOCUMENTS

There are three main avenues of approach to financial institutions. You can make an appointment to talk directly to your bank or building society manager, go to a mortgage broker and discuss your needs or investigate what's available on the internet.

When you go shopping for a mortgage remember that you have come to make a mutually beneficial deal, nothing more. You need a mortgage and the bank's business is to sell you one or more of its products. That's how they make their money. The more they lend you

and the greater the number and variety of insurance-based products
they manage to sell you, the more profit they make. It's a triumph of
marketing that some institutions manage to convince their customers
that they are doing them a favour by giving them a loan. However,
even though the amount you will be offered, or indeed whether you
are offered a loan at all, will depend on the hard facts of your
situation, it really does make a difference how you present your case.
The more businesslike you are, the more seriously you will be taken.
If you can show that you know what you are at, the process will be
much smoother.

Have a good idea of how much you are likely to be offered and
how you intend to pay it back before you apply for your loan. Have
as much as you can of the necessary documentation ready to hand in
order to avoid delays. Whether you deal directly with a lender,
through a broker or over the internet, your frustration threshold will
be reached very quickly as the amount of paperwork seems endless
unless you are prepared. Listed below are the documents you need
whichever route you take. Try to have them to hand *before* you start.

- As with any bank or building society account you need proof of
  identity to comply with the law. A passport or driver's licence
  with a photograph will suffice.
- As proof of your address you should bring a utility bill or some
  other official document addressed to you, such as a tax statement.
- A recent bank statement is normally asked for, though some
  lenders require three or four consecutive statements.
- You must have proof of permanent employment, such as a letter
  from your employer. If self-employed you should have three
  years' accounts. In addition, your most recent P60 from the
  Revenue Commissioners will generally be required.
- Finally, you may be asked for previous mortgage statements and
  details of any current personal borrowing, such as car loans or
  credit card debts, or some other indication that you have a good
  track record.

Armed with these documents you should be able to get an indication of
whether your application is likely to be successful and how much you
will be offered. This is of course merely an indication. A formal loan
offer will follow when all the necessary credit checks have been made.

HOW MUCH CAN YOU AFFORD?

The amount you can afford to pay for your home depends on how much you have saved and how much you can borrow. When you look for a mortgage, the success of your application depends on three factors: your income, relative to the amount you wish to borrow; your credit rating; and the value and condition of the property you hope to purchase. Today we can usually add a fourth, namely your ability to repay the loan. This involves more than just income and we will examine it in greater detail in Chapter 3.

Your Income

Most mortgage providers will advance about three times the annual income for an individual or three times the main income plus the second income for a couple. One of many variations offered by different institutions is 2.5 times the combined income of a couple, which generally gives a slightly higher figure.

Credit Rating

A history of bad debt, of having defaulted on other loans, may be recorded by credit-checking agencies. There is no point in being economical with the truth about your financial past, because (a) the lender may well find out about it and (b) it is against the law to obtain money under false pretences. If you have been declared bankrupt then, understandably, lenders will be reluctant to do business with you. From time to time we may hear about people who seem to be unable to secure credit and cannot understand why. It would appear that, occasionally, people of good standing end up being blacklisted by mistake, perhaps because of someone else's criminal activities. Legislation, passed in the late nineties, means that if you are refused a loan you are entitled to know if your credit rating has been compromised.

The Property

Many financial institutions will agree to lend up to 90 per cent, or even 92 per cent, of the value of the property you have in mind, assuming of course that you have sufficient income to cover the mortgage.

To ensure that the property is structurally sound, the institution will insist on a survey being carried out by its own surveyor,

something for which you must pay. The property must also be free from legal and planning difficulties. This usually means that there must be no extensions, conversions or changes of use for which planning permission is required, but has not been granted.

'Legal difficulties' generally refers to problems of title. One such common problem arises when a property is leasehold rather than freehold and there is only a short time left in the lease. 'Leasehold' means that the ground on which the property stands does not belong to the owner of the property but is vested in another and ground rent must be paid to that individual. Most leases are long-term, 999 years for example, and cause us no difficulties, as we are unlikely to be around by the time the lease is up. Older properties were sometimes set up on a 99-year lease and, while that might seem like a long time, such a property might now have less than 50 years left in the lease which is not enough to satisfy most mortgage providers.

Monthly Repayments

The most important thing to get right is your monthly repayment. The amount you pay depends on the term of the mortgage as well as the amount you borrow. Your monthly repayment should, ideally, be no more than one third of your net monthly income. It is difficult, long-term, to sustain a situation where a high proportion of your salary is swallowed up by your mortgage repayments – although it may be unavoidable for some borrowers at today's prices. The good news, however, is that while wages and salaries increase over time, fixed repayments don't, making the first year or two of repayments the hardest. An easy rule of thumb is that you can expect to pay – at current rates on an average mortgage – about €5 to €6 per €1,000 borrowed each month. This is only a very rough guide and levels will change in line with interest rate fluctuations and the term of the loan. Check the papers for the lowest rate available.

When considering the term of the loan there is a balancing act to be done. Take the loan on a longer term, say thirty years, and the repayments will be lower, but you will, of course, repay a great deal more in total over that time because of the extra interest involved.

YOUR MORTGAGE BROKER

If you are new to buying property I strongly urge you to find a good mortgage broker who has access to various types of loans from different financial institutions. He should also be someone you can talk to, who will listen to you and guide you through the wide selection of mortgages available. He is worth his weight in gold because the mortgage market is now so highly specialised that it is difficult for anybody but a professional in the field to be aware of the range of products available. An overview is useful, but you can benefit greatly by negotiating a loan which is tailored to your particular needs. A professional in the field will find the best option for you. Ask your family and friends who have already bought their homes and find out who they went to. Alternatively find a broker in the *Golden Pages*, but be sure you discuss your circumstances and the level of service offered. When you have a broker in mind, check that he is registered and find out how many institutions' products he can access. This is vital because many so-called mortgage advisors are agents for only one bank or building society. Ask if they charge a fee. Most don't because they get a commission from the lender, but do not be put off if there is a small charge. Everybody needs to make a living and by paying a small fee you may get a much better service.

Remember
A good mortgage broker is worth his weight in gold.

WHICH MORTGAGE?

It seems there are almost as many types of mortgage available as there are properties to buy and it can be daunting to evaluate them to ascertain which one suits you best. Many of these differences are, however, more apparent than real. Lenders go to great lengths to differentiate their products from those of their rivals. Broadly speaking, there are three main categories of mortgage, (a) the annuity mortgage, (b) the current account mortgage and (c) the endowment mortgage. Though popular at one time, the endowment mortgage fell out of favour when it failed to live up to its promise due to fluctuations in the stock market to which it was linked.

Other mortgage types such as *'interest-only'* are more suited to investors as they offer them tax advantages. These are discussed more fully in Chapter 9.

Currently the most popular type is the annuity mortgage.

However, there is another type of loan which is being actively marketed in Ireland that deserves a mention. This is the *'current account mortgage'*. It can be a blessing or a curse, depending on the level of discipline you can muster.

The Annuity Mortgage

This is the traditional type of mortgage. You make your repayments each month and in 20 or 30 years the house is yours, lock, stock and barrel. There is a great deal to be said for this type of loan, assuming some flexibility on the part of the lender. Each month you pay the interest on your loan plus some of the capital. In the early years most of the monthly payment is used to pay off the interest on the loan but, as the years go on, the amount paid as interest is less and a much higher amount is paid off the capital.

The Current Account Mortgage

The current account mortgage links both the mortgage and the borrower's current account. This means that any money sitting unused, even temporarily, in your current account is automatically paid into your mortgage, reducing your loan balance and thereby reducing your costs. Over the life of your loan it can save you thousands of euro. It works in reverse too. If you need extra cash at any time you can borrow from the equity stored in your property. This is the amount that you've already paid off relative to the market value. Usually up to 75 per cent of the current value is available as a loan.

This is a great idea for the virtuous! It can make a huge difference to how quickly you repay your loan in full as all lodgments are immediately credited to your account. The catch is that unless you're very disciplined you will be tempted to dip into your equity from time to time to pay for some of life's little luxuries. Unfortunately the upshot of this is that your are permanently in debt and you will never have the satisfaction of knowing that the roof over your head is totally yours and that nobody can take it away from you.

A good test to see if this mortgage is for you is to look at how you use your credit card. Do you pay your account in full each month, thus avoiding interest altogether? Or are you always playing *'catch up'*? If the latter and you were asking my advice about these loans, then I would suggest that you avoid them like a dose of dysentery.

OTHER CONSIDERATIONS
Interest: Fixed or Variable?
The price you pay for borrowed money varies over time and rates are currently at their lowest in 40 years. While property has never been so expensive, the cost of borrowing has never been so low. This has the great effect of making houses more affordable for a larger number of people. But buyer beware; rates can go up as well as down. I still have vivid memories of the mid-seventies when interest rates doubled in a year. I had just bought a second property to let and was hammered. (That was the year we had no holidays.) Fortunately there is now a mechanism to deal with such fluctuations as most lenders offer the choice of fixed rates, usually for one, three or five years. A fixed rate means that you know exactly how much you must pay each month on your mortgage. Regardless of how interest rates fluctuate on the open market, your rate will stay the same. When interest rates are low, it is a good time to consider going for a fixed rate. As the prospect of a rate increase becomes more likely, however, the fixed rate will rise. It is difficult to get the timing exactly right. Expect to pay slightly more than the variable rate for the security of a fixed loan.

Many borrowers are delighted with the peace of mind offered by a fixed rate. The downside – there's always something isn't there? – is that, if interest rates go down, you're still stuck at the higher rate. The other disadvantage is that if you wish to sell the property during the fixed period you will be subject to penalties. Check these out before you sign on the dotted line as they vary from one lender to another.

Discounted Rates
Lenders often offer discounted rates to first-time buyers and new customers. You should be aware, as it is not always clear, that these rates apply only to the first six or 12 months of the term of the mortgage. Be sure to check what you will be paying when the full rate becomes applicable. Other inducements and incentives offered to first-time buyers include things like free household insurance, free personal accident cover, etc. Examine the options and discuss the matter with your mortgage broker to find the offer that suits you best.

Flexibility
Can you alternate between fixed rate and variable should your circumstances change? Or alternatively can you pay off your loan in

full, without penalties, if you win the Lotto or inherit pots of money? These options are the essence of flexibility in mortgage terms. In addition, a wide range of goodies is offered to bring you on-side. These include items like *'deferred start'*, *'term reduction'*, *'low start'*, *'index linked'*, *'payment holidays'* and others. Again, check around but always remember that you still have to pay back the full amount and there's little point in putting it off. The process of checking is greatly speeded up if you have access to the internet as most mortgage providers set out their stalls on their websites where, if you submit your details, you will receive an instant quotation. However, it is not unusual to find that the quoted price doesn't apply in your particular case when a formal application is made.

For an examination of other mortgage options see Chapter 9.

Remember
Get it right first time.
Mistakes are very costly and not just in monetary terms – they place a strain on your health, your happiness and your relationships.

Mortgage Interest Tax Relief
This tax relief is available only on a mortgage taken out on your principal private residence. The relief is allowed at source by the lending institutions. This means that, once the relevant forms are completed, repayments are calculated after relief has been deducted. Currently the maximum amount of interest qualifying for tax relief is €2,540 for a single person and €5,080 for a married couple. At the time of writing the benefit of mortgage tax relief is €508 for a single person, €1,016 for a couple or a widowed person. First-time buyers enjoy a higher rate for the first seven years of their mortgage. This amounts to a credit of €800 for a single person and €1,600 for a couple or a widowed person. Mortgage Interest Tax Relief can be availed of in conjunction with various tax incentive schemes. Together they can dramatically reduce the amount spent on monthly repayments. One thing you need to know is that Mortgage Interest Tax Relief must be claimed for. In the past the relief was automatically deducted from the tax bill. Now a special form, obtained from the Revenue

Commissioners, must be completed and returned to them in order to avail of the allowance.

See Chapter 3 for an examination of tax-efficient property purchase for owner-occupiers.

FURTHER COSTS
Insurance
Most lending institutions now insist that purchasers take out a number of policies covering home insurance, mortgage payments and life assurance. These are to protect the institution in the event of the death of a borrower.

A lender will not release your mortgage cheque until you have buildings insurance in place. Life assurance is a legal requirement – and it is arguable whether you need both life assurance and mortgage protection. It really comes down to the level of security you are comfortable with. Be sure to shop around to get the best deal.

House insurance, is that all-important cover against the big nasties – fire, burglary, flood, subsidence – and, most importantly of all, in these litigious times, public liability. Its cost will obviously depend on the value of the property, but remember you are paying a premium per thousand euro according to the replacement value of the building, not the market price which includes the cost of the site. Though contents cover is generally not a requirement of lenders, it is in your own best interest to have your possessions insured in case something goes wrong. What may seem expensive now will be money well spent if disaster strikes. In addition, there is a public liability element of contents cover which is worth having. Without it you may not be insured if, for example, someone trips over a carpet in your house. Calculate the replacement value of all of your possessions and you will be surprised at just how much it comes to however modest your home.

Mortgage Repayment Policy
Cover should cost about 4.5 per cent of your repayment, that is €45 monthly on a mortgage costing €1,000. It is well worth paying for because of the peace of mind it brings. Read the small print to ensure you know what you are getting and that it is exactly what you want.

Surveys

In order to satisfy the lender that your house is not likely to fall down and is worth the purchase price, you will be required to have it surveyed by an independent assessor. The lender usually arranges this and it should cost you €120 to €150. It is separate from the structural survey that you should have done by your own engineer or architect. Though this could cost you up to €300, a good, independent structural survey can put your mind at rest about your chosen property. Not only will the property itself be evaluated, but also the surrounding area, alerting you to problems of traffic, pollution and proposed developments. You should get a detailed, written report which the surveyor will discuss with you, informing you of likely problems.

Legal Fees

Fees charged by your solicitor for conveyancing (that is the business of transferring the deeds of the property), dealing with the lender on your behalf and conducting all necessary searches and registration will amount to between €1,500 and €2,500 on an average property. Fees are usually calculated at 1 per cent of the purchase price of your property. Many solicitors are, however, willing to negotiate their fees. Discuss this in advance of any work being done on your behalf. A word of advice here – don't get too hung up on the price charged by professionals. Getting a satisfactory, professional job done is more important than saving a small amount of money. Like other businesses, solicitors have to be competitive to survive. As with your mortgage broker, choose someone you can get along with.

A group of solicitors attached to credit unions will carry out conveyancing at a flat rate of around €1,000 which can save you enough to have a modest holiday, something you will need when you've got to this stage. Check out Homebuy/Homesell either at your local Credit Union or at www.homebuyhomesell.ie. Have the holiday, you can buy that sofa anytime!

Stamp Duty

Of all the costs associated with purchasing property, stamp duty is the one that is most resented. The top rate is a whopping 9 per cent for a property over €635,000 with lower rates for lower priced houses (see Appendix 1). This duty (or tax) is collected by the government every time a property is sold. Today, as people move or re-mortgage on average every seven years, it brings millions of euro into the State's coffers and is without doubt among the most inequitable of taxes.

JOINT/GROUP PURCHASE

Financial institutions are now prepared to look more favourably than ever on the purchase of property by people who do not fall into the traditional pattern of purchasers, i.e. married couples or single people. When two or more people who are neither married to one another nor have close blood ties, decide to co-operate in the purchase of a property, certain formalities have to be adhered to. These rules commonly apply to cohabiting couples where both parties need to ensure that they contribute equally to funding the purchase, which will be owned jointly. This is necessary in order to ensure that no gift passes between them that might lead to a liability in respect of gift tax. To understand the thinking behind this reality, it is necessary to realise that cohabiting partners, as opposed to married ones, are strangers to each other in law. No gift tax or stamp-duty liability arises when property passes between spouses. Generally all Mortgage Interest Tax Relief which is due will be divided equally between the borrowers.

Remember
Now that you have sorted out your mortgage, you're more than halfway there.

Chapter 3
An Affordable Home

YOUR ABILITY TO REPAY

Look around you at all of the new houses and apartments being built. Only 10–20 per cent of them are being bought by investors. Ordinary people – nurses, people in banks, company reps and teachers – are buying the rest, in fact people very much like you and me. How do they do it? By making up their minds to do so and by taking all necessary steps to reach the goal they have set themselves, that's how. Like anything else in life that's worth having, this takes commitment and hard work. Alarming though the price increases of recent years are for someone trying to put a roof over their heads, they are not the full story. Do you remember the concept of *'affordability'* already mentioned? The real situation is not as bleak as many in the media would have us believe. Nowadays, the ability to repay your mortgage is at least as important as your income in determining the amount of a loan you will be offered. That sum also depends on a number of other factors, namely:

- your monthly income, minus your outgoings;
- the current mortgage interest rate;
- the level of borrowing you can live with;
- the value of any tax incentives available to you including mortgage interest relief;
- any income you can generate from your property; and
- any affordable housing schemes from which you can benefit.

'*Affordability*' is now a more important measure than just the price. Using the average manufacturing wage for a male worker and an average mortgage of €160,000 over 25 years which costs €9,800 p.a. to service, as a base, the affordability index equates with 33 per cent of his earnings. In the early eighties this ratio would have been over 38 per cent even though the average mortgage was only €23,000. This will come as no surprise to anyone who remembers interest rates of over 15 per cent at that time. The current, lower affordability index does not take into account the drop in income tax that has taken place since the early nineties. The combined impact of lower interest rates and taxes make repaying a loan much more comfortable than any time previously.

MONTHLY INCOME AND EXPENSES

Let's now have a look at your monthly income and outgoings to see how much you can repay each month. It is a good idea to work out your current monthly expenditure by totalling all of your bills, not forgetting to include sums for some non-essential but nonetheless necessary items like new clothes and a few just-for-fun things. Try not to overstretch yourself financially, but be prepared to make sacrifices for the first year or two to get started. It will be worth it in the end. After that things should get a little easier due to wage increases and the fact that you just get used to having less disposable income.

Net Monthly Income from All Sources

Don't forget in include *all* sources of income

Salary/Wages   ----------

Overtime Payments   ----------

Bonuses   ----------

Children's Allowances, etc.   ----------

Any other sources of income   ----------

Annual payments should be divided by twelve

Total   ----------

Monthly Outgoings

Rent ----------

Childcare ----------

Health Insurance ----------

Groceries ----------

Clothes ----------

Going Out ----------

Transport ----------

Telephone ----------

Mobile ----------

Clubs ----------

Charities ----------

Savings ----------

Loan Repayments ----------

House Insurance ----------

TV Licence ----------

Cable & Satellite ----------

Electricity ----------

Gas ----------

Life Insurance ----------

Home Maintenance ----------

Refuse Collection ----------

Total ----------

From this you can calculate the amount you can afford each month for your mortgage. There is a problem with this approach, however. Expenditure, for most of us, tends to be just in line with income, maybe a little below or a little above. Is it an immutable law of physics that expenditure always grows to swallow up all available income? When you have done your calculations, you will probably find that the amount available each month to cover a mortgage is nil. If this is your problem then you must take another look at your figures to see where you can make cuts in expenditure. Take 20 per cent off everything that is not fixed and then see how the final figure comes out. Twenty per cent is about the amount that can be shaved off most things with a little effort and economy. Some items such as satellite and cable TV are fixed and cannot be reduced. Decide whether you really need them. In general, you will feel less deprived if you make large savings where you can in one or two areas rather than to try to penny-pinch on everything. Can you, for example, do without a second car? Or do without any car? In this way you can make worthwhile savings without becoming obsessive.

TAX INCENTIVES FOR OWNER-OCCUPIERS

Your ability to repay your loan can also be enhanced in various ways. Most lenders will accept any additional income you can generate from the property, such as the rent from letting out a room, when calculating the amount you will be offered on your mortgage. See Chapter 4 for other ideas on making money from your home.

Another possibility to bring ownership of your own home within your grasp is to avail of one of the tax incentives which are still available to both owner-occupiers and investors. These, if you can use them, represent a good deal for prospective homeowners.

In a nutshell, in order to encourage development in certain designated areas in cities and some rural locations, the government gives generous concessions on income tax. This means that if you buy a home in one of these areas, up to 50 per cent of the price you pay will be allowable against your tax over a 10-year period. These concessions may be combined with Mortgage Interest Tax Relief. Unlike the latter, the tax relief is allowed at the taxpayer's top rate making the relief much more valuable. On the negative side, the government has designated these areas in order to encourage development in what are either fairly rundown inner-city areas or remote rural locations. Don't expect to find a designated area in a leafy suburb. To date these schemes have helped to revitalise inner-city areas that were derelict and have brought new life to some rural communities.

In summary the schemes, as they apply to owner-occupiers, are:

- **living over the shop**, which applies to certain designated areas of Dublin, Cork, Waterford, Limerick and Galway.
- **rural renewal scheme**, which is available in counties Leitrim and Longford and certain parts of Cavan, Roscommon and Sligo.
- **town renewal scheme**, which applies in various towns around the country.
- **integrated area plan scheme**, which applies in areas of Cork, Waterford, Galway and Limerick cities.

An allowance of 50 per cent on the capital cost of the property, less the cost of the site, is given to the owner-occupier. In the case of refurbished properties, this allowance is 100 per cent, again less site costs. The income-tax allowance is spread over 10 years. One thing to be aware of, however, is that site costs can be quite high in inner-city areas and this may significantly reduce the amount of qualifying expenditure.

For a full list of Tax Incentive Schemes and their cut-off dates, see Appendix 2.

WHAT IF MY INCOME IS LOW?

It used to be the case that buyers were reluctant to borrow up to the limit of what they were offered as a mortgage because they were afraid of being over committed. As credit levels explode, and are now many times that of just a few years ago, this attitude seems about as outmoded as woodchip wallpaper and Beautyboard. Economic commentators are now suggesting that, like the rest of the developed world, the Irish are getting used to the idea of being permanently in debt. Call me naïve (and I know it's not part of my brief in this book to discuss broader economic issues) but at some point hard questions will have to be asked about just who benefits from the current system. In the meantime, we can look at the several options available to those on low incomes.

AFFORDABLE HOUSING SCHEMES

In 1999 the first Local Authority Affordable Housing Scheme was set up, giving thousands of people the opportunity to purchase houses below the market price and within their means. It was aimed at nurses, junior doctors, teachers and others whose incomes might fall below that needed to buy a house at market rates in some areas but were too high to allow them to avail of local authority public housing. A year later, with the implementation of Part V of the Planning and Development Act 2000, this scheme really took off.

Under its provisions developers were required to make 20 per cent of private developments available to local authorities to be sold at cost price to qualifying purchasers, many of whom would never otherwise have been able to own their homes. Further a 2002 amendment to the original act gave builders the option of providing a cash or land equivalent to actual housing units. This gave the local authorities somewhat more flexibility in the implementation of the schemes, though some have argued that it let the developers off the hook. It also meant that the available housing units were situated in less attractive areas, often far from the places most people wanted to live.

Those eligible to benefit under the original scheme include the following.

- First-time buyers in single-income households whose gross income did not exceed €32,000 in 2002.
- Double-income households whose combined gross income (based on the formula 2.5 times the larger salary and once the smaller income) did not exceed €80,000 in 2002. Check your local authority for the up-to-date income figures.

To reduce the cost to the purchaser further, the local authority may apply for a subsidy to the Department of the Environment & Local Government. This makes these schemes very attractive indeed to buyers. Perhaps the main drawback is that, should the buyer decide to sell the house within a 10-year timeframe, the authority will claim back the difference between the cost price and the market value of the property. In years 10 to 20 the amount of the claw-back is reduced each year by 10 per cent, so that if, the house is sold after 20 years, the profit goes entirely to the vendor.

Under what is commonly termed '*Part V Provision*', arising from the Planning & Development acts 2000 and 2002, anyone whose mortgage payments exceed 35 per cent of their annual net income may apply for Affordable Housing. In 2003 under the Sustaining Progress Affordable Housing Initiative, the government announced the provision of up to 10,000 housing units within the schemes, mainly in urban areas.

Confused? You are not alone. Due to the fact that there are now three separate schemes in existence, I wonder if anybody in the country has a clear understanding of just who is eligible to benefit. However, the 2004 provision for capital spending on social and affordable schemes is €1.885 billion – an increase on the figure of €1.7 billion spent in 2003 – and a total of 12,500 households are expected to benefit from this expenditure. It is to be hoped that supply will not continue to be an issue. Only 153 of the 63,000 new homes built last year were in the *social and affordable homes* bracket. Although some authorities are taking time to come to grips with the red tape, it is important to remember they are legally bound to provide the schemes.

Social Housing
In addition to the measures outlined above, the following schemes are also available to those on low incomes. Some are specifically tailored to suit the needs of local authority tenants, though others could benefit anybody whose income is low.

Shared Ownership
This scheme is designed for those on low or middle incomes who would not qualify for a full mortgage in the private market. A couple could have an income of around €52,000 annually and still qualify for this scheme. Under the terms of the scheme the purchase of the property is financed by a combination of a mortgage and rent paid to the council. This scheme seems to work well for some people. The applicant initially owns a minimum of a 40 per cent share in the property and rents the remainder from the local authority with an undertaking to buy out the remaining 60 per cent within 25 years. Any house or apartment will quality for this scheme provided the council is satisfied that it is reasonably priced, of suitable size and of standard construction. The applicant's share of the property will normally be funded by way of a mortgage from the local authority. These

mortgages are very competitive at 3.55 per cent per annum. The other 60 per cent of the ownership may be acquired by purchasing the remaining shares from time to time. The cost will be the initial purchase price adjusted annually to compensate for fluctuations in interest rates. This may be financed by an additional mortgage, again provided by the local authority.

There are two important things to note here. The initial capital value (i.e. the price at which the property was bought) is the value used when buying out the local authority's share. The property is deemed to increase only by the consumer price index. Second, there is no obligation to repay all the outstanding capital on the mortgage within the 25 years. This can be accomplished by way of a second mortgage. The net effect is a longer period in which to buy the property, making the repayments even more manageable for those on lower incomes. Perhaps the greatest advantage of this scheme is that the deposit needed is low. Many people have done very well on this scheme. The only drawback in this scheme appears to be that if you want to sell the property it can be difficult to extricate yourself from the arrangement.

Let's look at an example of how the scheme works in practice.

Cost of property, including professional fees	€300,000
Value of the 40% owned by the applicant	€120,000
Deposit (purchaser's savings) of 10%	€30,000
Mortgage	€90,000
Value of the 60% owned by the local authority	€180,000

House Purchase Loans
These loans are advanced by local authorities to people on low and middle incomes who have been unable to secure a mortgage privately. They can be used in conjunction with the other schemes outlined here. They are not confined to local authority tenants but are open to all.

Tenant Purchase
This scheme, operated by local authorities, enables a tenant to purchase the house or flat they already occupy. Under the current arrangements, tenants who hold a tenancy for at least a year can avail of a discount of 3 per cent per year up to 30 per cent of the market value of the property after 10 years in occupation and also qualify for an additional grant.

Mortgage Allowance

Tenants and tenant purchasers who hand back their existing dwellings to their local authority in order to buy privately may avail of a subsidy towards their mortgage repayments. This subsidy is payable over five years. The amount of the subsidy depends on income levels and is at the discretion of the local Community Welfare Officer.

Low-Cost Housing Sites

Local authorities may provide housing sites from their own land banks at low cost to people in need of housing. This scheme can be availed of, in conjunction with the others outlined above, by those who qualify. Each application is judged individually on its merits. The main constraint to the operation of this scheme is the availability of land.

On paper the schemes outlined above look very impressive. In practice their implementation is patchy. Cash-strapped local authorities don't appear to have the resources to target the people who could benefit most from them.

Contact the housing section of your local authority for further information on any of these schemes. In many cases persistence and perseverance will win out. The schemes are there, but often local authority staff, already overworked, won't encourage people to avail of them.

FINDING THE DEPOSIT

There is a dream shared by many, where the dreamer is rowing a small boat against the current of a fast river. No matter how hard he tries, he can't get anywhere because the current is always faster than he can row. But he has to keep on rowing or he will go over the cliff and be wrecked. And the cliff is getting nearer and nearer all the time. Saving for a house can be a bit like that, if less dramatic.

You need 10 per cent of the cost of the house as a deposit but, as you save, the price of the property is escalating much faster than your ability to put the 10 per cent together. Instead of coming closer to your goal it quickly disappears over the horizon. Prices, certainly in recent years, have always outpaced the ability of most would-be home-owners to save. How to escape from the trap? It would be extremely foolish of me to pretend to have easy answers to this one. If you cannot, for whatever reason, avail of the shared ownership scheme outlined above then the suggestions below should help you to broaden your perspective – to think outside the box – and find a solution.

Looking to Your Strengths

- Are you well informed? Many lenders will now give 92–93 per cent loans. One newcomer to the market is, at time of writing, offering 100 per cent loans to clients in certain professions.
- Do you have a friend or relative willing to act as a guarantor with a lender for you? If so, it is possible to get an almost 100 per cent loan on your mortgage, especially if that person has a property which could be used as collateral. Beware, however, of overstretching yourself when it comes to the monthly repayments!
- Do you have a friend, or a number of friends, in the same position? Today it is reasonably easy for a group of friends to get a joint loan whereas in the past this was something confined to married couples. The great advantage of this approach is that in a few years you will be able to sell the property, leaving each of you with a sizeable deposit for a home of your own. Take care, however, to make sure that there is absolute clarity about how the arrangement works. You must have an exit mechanism in place should one person want to opt out due to a change of circumstances or for any other reason. Tease these matters out with your solicitor and have him draw up an agreement to be signed by all of you. You will most likely be charged very little, if anything at all, for this facility if you use the same solicitor for the purchase of the property.
- Do you have family members who would lend you some of the money? Do not use this as your first option. If you have been seen to be saving and doing your best to achieve your goal on your own, others will be much more sympathetic and inclined to help you. Some might be persuaded by an offer to pay interest on the loan, perhaps even a slightly higher rate than the banks, while others would be insulted at such a suggestion. As with friends, take care with your family. No property, no money, nothing, is worth the suffering and pain caused all round if you fall out with your family. If they help you it is out of the goodness of their hearts and you should be very grateful. Be careful how you

broach the subject. Be open and honest and you will gain respect. You could have a solicitor draw up an agreement to be signed by both parties, though do bear in mind that many older people would find the formality of making arrangements through a solicitor very intrusive.

- What about earning some extra money? Everyone has some skills that someone else will pay for. Can you type, wait on tables or help in a shop? What about cleaning, babysitting or sitting with an elderly person? Could you write letters, articles, do some gardening, painting or wall papering? Are you good at handcrafts, knitting, sewing or garment alterations? Could you make beautiful dresses for weddings or First Communions? Are you proficient at book-keeping, bee-keeping or computers? All of these skills are in great demand. I have deliberately avoided those which have special requirements not available to most people, such as regulation kitchens for food preparation or building work which involves having a safety pass. If you have a trade, consider yourself lucky as you are unlikely to be short of work in the foreseeable future. Usually all you need to do is to place a few advertisements in local papers to get started. Evening papers, if they are available in your area, usually advertise services cheaply, sometimes at no charge.

- Consider also the assets you already possess and make a list. Do you have a car? Can you do without it for a while? Consider how much it is worth and how much you can save on running costs if you sell it. Do you have an expensive stereo system? How much would you get for it? Have you other valuable, disposable assets? When you begin to list them you will be surprised at how rich you are.

- Is it feasible to move back home for a while to give yourself a bit of extra saving power? Once again, don't take your parents for granted.

If all of this effort and sacrifice seems daunting don't forget that it's only temporary. Your reward will be the joy of having your own place. You may not believe it now, but when you succeed, the pride in your achievement, the knowledge that you have succeeded at something difficult but worthwhile, will be at least as important to you as the property itself.

PARENTAL ASSISTANCE IN BUYING YOUR HOME

Are you in line to inherit cash or property? If so, then maybe your parents or other relatives would be willing to gift it to you now. Many parents do this today as they realise how difficult it is for their children to get started. Again, do not be presumptuous. Your parents have probably worked hard for what they have. They are entitled to spend it on themselves in their advancing years. However, many are happy to help out, making things easier for their children and gaining the satisfaction of seeing their families enjoying the fruits of their labours within their own lifetimes. You may remember a year or two ago that a major building society ran a series of television and radio advertisements where a grown-up son approached his father, asking him to put his house on the line as security for the son's mortgage. There was such a strong public reaction of outrage that the advertisements had to be withdrawn. It would be very interesting to work out why the public reacted so negatively, but that's for another day.

Assistance from parents can take many forms. Often money is given directly to a son or daughter, or help may take the form of acting as a guarantor for a loan. There may, however, be implications for the recipients in the form of gift tax or stamp duty. Though in recent years special reliefs (outlined below) from these taxes have been introduced to make it easier for parents to help, it is important not to simply ignore these considerations, but to discuss them with a financial advisor who is expert in this area. (See also Chapter 11.)

Taxation Implications of Parental Assistance

- Acting as guarantor for a mortgage for a son or daughter has no taxation implications.
- A site, up to a certain value, to be used for private residence may be transferred, free of taxes, from parent to child.
- A gift of a residence to a child who has been living there for the past three years incurs no tax liabilities if the child continues to live there for a further six years.
- Parents are entitled to make tax-free gifts of cash to their children up to a lifetime limit of, at time of writing, €456,438. An interest-free loan is regarded as a benefit and can use up part of the lifetime allowance. Cash gifts should always be made directly to the child of the parent and not to the child and partner as the gift-tax threshold is much lower for those other than the

offspring. A son or daughter's spouse or partner could incur a tax liability if a substantial gift were made to them as a couple.

- Parents sometimes purchase property in a child's name and let it until the child comes of age.
- Other legal mechanisms involve Deeds of Trust. Such arrangements require specialised legal advice which you can get from your solicitor.

By now I hope you are beginning to see some possibilities at least of advancement towards your goal. In Chapter 4 we will look at some of the ways in which you can make money from your home. Don't forget that, depending on your lender, *all* sources of income may be taken into account when applying for a mortgage.

Chapter 4

Making Money from Your Home

There is an Old Irish proverb, *'Is measa ná muc fear gan seift'* (which literally translates as: *'A man without a plan is worse than a pig'*). What a shame to insult lovely, pink pigs who are most intelligent animals. But of course the real meaning is that there should always be a plan B. Do you, at the back of you mind, have any idea of what you would do if everything went pear shaped? As a young woman I used to put money aside in the toes of my second best boots – just in case, because you never know! Having friends in Barcelona, I always had the idea that I could go there and teach English if the worst happened (though I was always too scared to define the worst). It's always reassuring to know what you would do to get yourself out of a tight spot. View this chapter in that light. Many of you don't need to give a moment's thought to any of the strategies suggested here, having plenty of money at you disposal. In fact, you can skip it altogether if you are flush with cash and blessed with an impervious sense of security – you lucky devil.

There are several ways of making money from your home. Some or them are:

- renting out a room or two;
- taking in a paying guest;
- working from home; and
- setting up as a B&B.

Strategies to make money from your home fall into two main categories: (a) options to be used when money is a little tight such as when you need a bit extra to get you through the first few years of a mortgage, these are of a temporary nature, and (b) opportunities which, if taken, may mean a radical change of lifestyle.

For an increasing number of people buying a particular home is part of a larger re-orientation of their lives. Some, by working from home, hope to combine family and work in a more relaxed way than the long, daily commute to a high-pressure job allows. Often such people have a qualification or expertise which lends itself to home-working. Occupations such as writing, teaching, counselling and many others fall into this category. For other people, the impetus to make a fundamental shift comes directly from a hobby or special interest and a dream of independent living free from the constraints of the clock and the traffic.

RENTING OUT A ROOM OR TWO

Privacy means different things to different people. What one person considers an intolerable intrusion is a lively, friendly presence to another. In my own case, I grew up in the midst of a family business where home and the shop happily co-existed on the same premises. As children we could never do normal things like coming downstairs in the mornings in our nightclothes, as there was usually a commercial traveller or a staff member taking a tea break in our living room, which doubled as a staff meeting room. It would be difficult to imagine a livelier, more stimulating place to grow up, but it took me years to appreciate that not everyone was as casual about personal and family boundaries. Others I lived with later on had totally different ideas about personal space and couldn't conceive of living in a place with so many outsiders coming and going that it sometimes resembled Heuston Station on a Friday evening.

If you are considering taking outsiders into your home be sure to weigh up the pros and cons carefully in advance, and unless you live alone discuss it with your family. Letting out a room is a good idea, especially if your spare room has an en-suite bathroom, though this is not essential.

My friend May, a retired nurse, lives near the offices of a large corporation and has been renting her spare room for almost 10 years now. Her tenants are company employees on six-month contracts. Technicians and engineers in the main, they are settled men who leave their homes in the UK to come here alone because the term of their contacts is too short to uproot their families. At weekends they generally return home, leaving May with an empty house, free to enjoy entertaining her friends. It is a very satisfactory arrangement on both sides. May has company in the house, which she enjoys, an extra income which is very welcome and her tenant has all of the comforts of a lovely home at a modest price. Her tenants do their own cooking and cleaning. A natural gift for communication and the ability to make her rules very clear right from the start in the nicest, but firmest, possible way mean that May's arrangements always seem to work like a dream.

It is important that all parties to this type of arrangement know just what is expected of them, so rules have to be spelled out. Once the ground rules have been established things can, ideally, be relaxed and informal and an atmosphere of give-and-take can become the norm. The fact that May has enjoyed a marked lack of friction between her renters and herself can be put down to her common sense, tolerance and flexibility.

When things go wrong between people sharing accommodation it usually begins with a dispute over one of a few basic issues, such as:

- smoking;
- cooking;
- cleaning;
- bills;
- maintenance;
- telephone;
- the living room;
- visitors;
- pets; and
- deposits.

Once you are clear on what is and what is not acceptable to you then you can explain this clearly to someone else. The biggest mistake homeowners make in this situation is that they are over-accommodating at the start and try to row back later.

Smoking

It never ceases to amaze me how strongly people feel about smoking. Yes, I know all about the health hazards, but I do think all sense of proportion has gone out of the window when it comes to this issue. It seems to be the number one irritant, *guaranteed* to cause friction between those on both sides of the argument. Do you mind people smoking in your home? If you have no objection in principle will you mind them smoking in their bedrooms or in the living room? Do you smoke yourself? If so would you be willing to confine yourself to smoking in maybe one room only to accommodate another person's preference? If you think smoking might cause problems for you maybe you should search for a tenant who has the same attitude as yourself. As with the other issues, there is no right or wrong answer. These are not moral conundrums. The important thing is to decide where you stand on potentially contentious issues.

Cooking

When someone rents a room in a house they do not expect to be waited on hand and foot nor do they expect to have a live-in cook. In most cases the renter is given a space in the fridge for his food. He will, of course, expect access to the kitchen when he wishes to cook. Some items such as milk or washing-up liquid can be shared. Perhaps each person could put €5 or €10 each week into a jar on the kitchen window to cover these items. However, rights always bring responsibilities, so it should be made clear to the cook that he should clean up afterwards.

Cleaning

This can be a difficult one. As with the cooking, the one who makes the mess should be the one who sorts it out. Common sense should prevail when it comes to household chores such as cleaning communal bathrooms. But don't be surprised if nobody will clean your house as thoroughly as you would yourself. There is a thin line between expecting someone to take legitimate responsibility for his share of the work and imposing your own standards on others, but a line does exist and it's important to find it. Even many married couples have difficulties with this one, so I'm not naïve enough to try, in this limited space, to give you a definitive answer to how it should be handled.

Bills

In a house share or *'rent a room'* arrangement utility bills – gas, electricity, etc. – are usually divided between the occupiers of the house, but the arrangement that works best is the one that all parties are comfortable with. Renters often prefer to know just where they stand, how much they must pay each week or month. It should be possible to agree a figure that will be acceptable to both sides and include it in the rent.

Maintenance

Upkeep of the premises will usually be the responsibility of the owner. An exception would be where the renter caused some damage to the property or to items such as furniture. Common sense would dictate that the person who causes damage would be liable for the repairs necessary to make good that damage. But don't rely on common sense – make sure the tenant understands what he is liable for.

Telephone

Nowadays the telephone is less of an issue than previously as most people have a mobile phone. Some arrangement must be made, however, regarding the use of a landline phone. Renters would not expect to have the use of the landlord's phone. Coin operated phones used to offer a good solution to this problem but they seem to be less readily available today. Perhaps the simplest way to avoid disputes is for the landlord and the renter to have landlines in their own bedrooms.

The Living Room

The living room can be the most contentious issue of all. It can be difficult for people to agree on whether the TV should be on, what programmes to watch, etc. Ideally, if the house is large enough, and if you have more than one renter, a second living room should be considered. Alternatively, as with the phone, a tv in each bedroom is the answer. This is not to suggest that the property owner should, in his own home, be as restricted as the tenant, but it is wise to guard against the build-up of resentments, yours or others.

Entertaining

How do you feel about your tenant having visitors? Are you willing to abide by whatever rule you consider reasonable for your tenant? If your place is small, it might not be realistic to have other than occasional casual callers except on rare occasions or when you have the place to yourself. A more difficult question is how do you feel about your tenant having someone to stay overnight?

Pets

I think most people would agree that it would be very unusual for someone who is renting a room in your home to expect to be able to bring in a pet. However, it has been known to happen, sometimes to the dismay of the owner of the house. Some animal lovers on the other hand would welcome others' pets.

Deposits

As with renting a flat or house, a deposit equal to three or four weeks' rent would be advisable, though many people find it unnecessary. This is for the homeowner to keep in case damage is caused or to cover non-payment of rent. Some landlords are reluctant, without cause, to refund deposits when the renter wishes to leave. This practice is both illegal and unfair. The renter is entitled to a refund in full of his deposit if no damage or breakages have occurred and he or she can make a claim against the landlord for a full deposit refund in the Small Claims Court on payment of a nominal fee. Damage should not be confused with wear and tear which is part of what is paid for in the rent.

TAKING IN A PAYING GUEST

The word *'digs'* has probably as many negative associations as the word *'landlord'*. It conjures up hard-faced landladies who know the price of everything, even harder beds and a pervasive smell of boiled cabbage. It differs from renting out a room because meals are usually provided as in a guesthouse. If you have the space and time to cook daily then you can make a significant income from a few guests. First year, third-level students, fresh from home, often feel safer in digs than in flatland. (Or perhaps it's their mothers who prefer them to have the closest thing they can find to the security and comfort of home.) Business people too, who have to spend a few weeks or nights away from home on a regular basis, are often attracted to the idea of a cooked meal waiting for them in the evening. If you are inviting others to share your home be sure to take all the precautions you can in order to get it right. Do not, on any account, be blasé about security. Have locks fitted on all of the bedroom doors and on any areas of the house you wish to keep private for your own use. It is important to have this done before anyone moves in as doing it later might cause resentment.

Apply to local colleges in plenty of time for students seeking digs. While college courses usually begin in September or October, accommodation offices generally compile their lists several months in advance.

Taking a paying guest into your home became easier when the Minister for Finance relaxed the rules on taxation in 2001. Since then a homeowner is permitted to earn up to €7,260 in annual rent, the provision of meals, etc. without incurring any tax liability. Under the Residential Tenancies Act 2004, a property owner who lets rooms in a premises in which he himself resides is specifically excluded from the obligations of a landlord as set out in the act. This means there is no onus on the householder to register as a landlord. It also means that the renter won't acquire any of the rights of a tenant. It is a good idea to inform your insurance company of your intention, but there is unlikely to be any additional premium to be paid.

Finding the Right Person
In view of the fact that you will be living closely with the person who shares your home, great care should be devoted to finding the right person. Like my friend, May, you could confine your search to one large organisation, though this might not be sufficient to ensure a steady stream of guests. Don't forget hospitals and second-level schools. Your best initial approach is to telephone the organisation in question and ask permission to post a notice on the staff notice board. Be sure to get the name of the person to whom you are speaking, it will then be easier to enter the building without running the risk of being unceremoniously ejected by security! Have your notice ready in advance stating where you live and what you have to offer. In the interest of security never give your full address or any personal details. Especially, do not suggest that you live alone. If you don't have access to a computer and printer at home or work, get a friend to print your notice or go to a business centre or library as it will look a lot more businesslike than a badly written legend on a piece of cardboard. Put your phone number on it, preferably a mobile, as you don't want to

be stuck at home, waiting for replies. Using little strips that can be torn off one by one is a useful way to encourage people to take your number.

As well as posting your notice in nearby offices and factories, tell everyone you know that you are looking for someone. Word of mouth is the best possible recommendation on both sides. If after all of this strenuous activity your efforts have failed to produce a tenant within a reasonable timespan, your next strategy should be to advertise in the local papers. Anti-discrimination laws preclude you from advertising specifically for a male or a female. It is against the law to discriminate against people on nine different counts: race, religion, marital status, family status, age, sexual orientation, gender, disability and membership of the Travelling Community.

When someone telephones you in response to the advert don't be afraid to ask as many questions as you deem fit to help you decide whether you want this person in your home. Find out, in a friendly and polite but firm way, where the caller works and in what capacity, where he is staying currently and why he is leaving there. Explain that you will require three references and a deposit. If you are happy with the response you get then you can give the caller your address and arrange a time for him to visit your home. Get a name and telephone number in case you need to cancel because you have let the room to someone else. I cannot emphasise strongly enough the importance of having another person present when perspective renters call. You can never be too careful, so call in the favour you did for your friend or sister, or your first cousin once removed, and have someone else in your house with you. If other family members or renters stay in the home it might be a good idea to include them in the discussions to see how everybody gets along. This is the time to make sure of the ground rules and to draw up a written agreement if necessary.

HOME-BASED WORK

Way back in the early seventies in a book entitled *Future Shock*, Alvin Toffler wrote imaginatively about what he called '*the technological cottage*'. It was, even then, a feasible way to combine work and home life without the stress of the daily commute and the drama of trying to find emergency childcare at 8 a.m. when your childminder rings in sick.

Many jobs lend themselves to working from home, for example:

- information technology;
- childminding;
- hairdressing;
- writing;
- craft work; and
- accountancy.

The list is endless. Type in *'work from home'* on the internet, click and watch the plethora of opportunities that appear. Most of them are of course duds, especially the ones that promise you vast sums for a few hours work a week. But you only need one good idea to turn into a successful business. Many ideas can be adapted and can work. I know of one woman who publishes a diet on the internet. She claims no particular expertise in the fields of diet or nutrition beyond what most of us has – the experience of trying every diet under the sun. She sells her diet at €15 for a printable copy and ongoing support. It is full of practical tips and I'm told it works as a diet and that she makes a not insignificant income from it. Another friend has erected one of those new timber room-type structures in his garden, a kind of superior shed. Here he has set up a thriving pottery business, a one-man operation producing beautiful objects, which are greatly sought-after.

Making a living at home, or pursuing a part-time occupation, assuming you have sufficient space in which to operate, is a very efficient use of resources which enables you to avoid the cost or alternative premises such as an office or a workshop. Many of the world's biggest enterprises, Microsoft for example, began life in sheds. There are probably hundreds of small enterprises going on right now in garages and spare bedrooms, which will be the business giants of tomorrow. How many musical outfits, which began life as garage bands, have made it to the world stage, I wonder? A garden shed or spare room may be ideal for your enterprise, but often a kitchen table will suffice. If, however, you need public access, to be available to clients, then there are insurance implications, so inform your broker or insurance company of your intentions.

SETTING UP A B&B
Although similar to digs, setting up a B&B business is a more formal and larger enterprise. You will need plenty of space and standards

have to be professional. Many travellers love to stay in bed and breakfasts. Americans, in particular, like the warmth and personal touch, the feeling of being part of a family that a B&B can offer. Lone travellers, in particular, often feel less isolated here than in the impersonal atmosphere of a big hotel. It is impossible, however, to give definite guidelines here regarding planning permission, fire regulations and so on as these are technical matters which need to be examined with the help of an engineer and other advisers. In addition, larger enterprises must be registered for VAT. A good accountant will advise you on the business matters. Once again, don't forget the insurance implications. It is necessary to talk to your broker and to discuss appropriate cover. The main difficulty you will face is the setup cost. The installation of additional bathrooms and fire protection can be very expensive, depending on the layout of your house.

You have to be fairly well organised and good at keeping records to run a successful bed and breakfast. Many B&B businesses become affiliated to the Irish Tourist Board as this practically guarantees business. You can, if you wish, remain independent and many do so because of the exacting standards and unannounced inspections imposed on them by the tourist board. This is not, in any way, to condone lower standards, but some businesses find that the regulations do not match their own priorities in providing good-quality accommodation. The good news is that in setting up the business you are in a position to renovate and decorate your property, claiming at least some of your costs as a legitimate business expense. Once again, don't forget to inform your insurance company of what you are doing. This is essential, as you will need extra insurance cover for public liability.

Running a successful guesthouse, however small, would warrant a book of its own, but there are a few suggestions that you might find useful.

• Situation is important with any business. Ideally you should be located in a spot where there is a passing trade and a sign will bring in business. You may, however, need planning permission for the sign. You can still succeed even if you are in a remote place. Market your operation as a quiet hideaway, or a place for healthful weekends and decorate it to suit. People will come to you again and again if you are good enough, though you have to try a lot harder if you are off the beaten track.

- Be sure you approach local hotels and other larger guesthouses, asking them to keep your card to hand. Most establishments like to be able to recommend an alternative to customers if they are full. If you offer a good service and a few extra touches, word of mouth will soon see you doing well.
- Most guests expect a full, cooked breakfast. Don't expect to get away with anything less than good food that is cooked well.
- Have good, new beds if you expect repeat business.
- Your home has to be spotless; bathrooms must always be gleaming and kitchens pristine. This is not a job for those who hate housework.
- Finally, the décor in your home should be comfortable though not shabby. Only in large houses with pretensions to being historic will you get away with tat.

Chapter 5
Completing the Purchase

DEALING WITH ESTATE AGENTS AND SOLICITORS

Patience is a virtue, they say, and I hope you have it in bucketfuls. You have found the home of your dreams, or at least the best you can afford, your mortgage has been arranged and you are ready to roll, wanting everything sorted in jig time. This is when you need patience. It's frustrating, but at least you have been warned. Like the expectation of a good summer, to think the practicalities will go without a hitch is bordering on delusional. In theory, it should take about 28 days from *'sale agreed'* to *'sold'* but I have yet to buy a property that didn't throw at least one wobbly. Sometimes it's the mortgage. I once found myself on my way to do the weekly shopping, at half-past four on a Friday afternoon, with rain pouring down like the day of the Flood, two small children in tow, and expecting six guests for dinner in a couple of hours. I had just been informed by phone that the mortgage company required extra documentation before five thirty that afternoon so that a sale could be closed first thing on Monday morning. The vendor, I was told, would pull out of the deal if all was not ready. All the organisation the world doesn't ensure that that sort of thing won't happen. Sometimes the sale doesn't get to first base because the seller pulls out. Often the buyer finds that he has difficulties getting the mortgage sanctioned.

The legalities of buying a property can be confusing and frustrating for first-time buyers. Those who are not buying their first home will have the advantage of having been through the mill at least once before. But the process becomes a feat of logistics and perseverance on the scale of a polar expedition when trying to synchronise the sale of an existing home and the purchase of a new property. I cannot understand why this is so difficult. It should, in theory, run smoothly when the groundwork has been done meticulously, but many people seem to have an awkward patch between homes, when they are forced to seek alternative accommodation.

Choosing a solicitor is one of the few relatively straightforward things when it comes to buying your house. Virtually all solicitors are experienced in conveyancing as this activity is the bread and butter of most legal practices. Many first-time buyers simply trot along to the solicitor used by their parents when they bought their own houses. That said, it could be worthwhile to shop around, as there are young solicitors out there, new to the business, who are willing to be very flexible and competitive on price. A young couple I know who recently bought their first home were delighted to find a solicitor willing to meet them at weekends, even on a Sunday, as they worked long hours during the week and would have found it difficult to take time off for consultations. Solicitors traditionally charge a percentage of the purchase price of the property, though some ask considerably less. Don't be afraid to negotiate. Don't forget the alternative option mentioned in Chapter 2, of using the Credit Union scheme offering conveyancing for a flat fee of around €1,000.

Pity the poor estate agent. Like landlords, agents have had a bad press. No matter how much they try to provide a good, professional service, very few people give the hard-working agent the recognition he deserves. Whatever your feelings about them, you need to make friends with yours now. Knowledge of a few basic realities will help put your relationship with estate agents on a sound footing. First, the agent is not working for you, but for the seller. Don't forget that '*he who pays the piper calls the tune*', so the agent's loyalties are to his client. Second, never expect an agent to ring you when a property which might meet your needs comes on the market. There are, typically, more potential buyers than properties, so that if the agent chases you, you can be reasonably sure that the property in question is difficult to sell. When working as an agent myself I began with the admirable idea that I would follow up every potential purchaser until

I found something suitable for him or her. I very quickly realised that this was a complete waste of time. Most people had found a place, dropped out of the market or gone away when I returned to them. It's up to you to keep in touch with the agents and prove that you are a serious buyer.

VIEWING A PROPERTY

Going to visit properties you cannot afford, or in which you have no real interest, is a nice pastime. Nothing whatsoever wrong with it – but, like using a €2,000 computer to play patience, it is a waste of a valuable resource, which in this case is time. It is the property market's equivalent of what those in the motor trade call *'tyre kickers'* and is guaranteed to get up the noses of estate agents. If you expect to be taken seriously don't do it. Before arranging to view a property, study the brochure. Look especially at the room sizes and where they are relative to one another if there is a floor plan. Drive around the area in which the property is situated if you don't already know it. Satisfy yourself that it fits your budget. Have a look at a map of the area and don't be afraid to ask the agent as many questions as you wish. Asking questions will save everybody a lot of time spent viewing unsuitable properties. Have a checklist, such as the one below, so that you are neither put off by a bit of mess nor seduced by something that catches your eye, such as the owner's plants or his taste in music.

Remember
Be ready to buy before you view.

Checklist

What is the state of the:	
Outside	*Inside*
Plaster?	Windows?
Brickwork?	Timber?
Chimneys?	Floors?
Roof?	Kitchen units?
Driveway?	Bathroom?
Drains?	Plaster?
Garden?	

Add the following to your checklist.

- Is there an extension? If so, how is it constructed?
- What type of heating is there?
- Is there evidence of damp or dry rot?
- Has the place been done up recently in an effort to hide its faults?
- Do the electrics look modern and safe or are they decrepit?
- Are there enough rooms and are they of reasonable size?
- Will the smallest bedroom be big enough to take a full-sized single bed?
- Is there enough storage space? Nowadays people accumulate so many possessions that ample storage is an essential in every home.
- Is the property good enough to live in as it is, or will it need extensive decoration or even refurbishment?
- Is there off-street parking? If not, is the street parking adequate?
- What about the view? A nice view is a great asset, but don't forget that it can be enhanced by good planting in the garden.

Factor in all additional costs associated with the property: stamp duty, ground rent and legal fees. Ongoing expenses should also be considered. If it is an apartment, management charges and contingency fund contributions must not be forgotten.

If refurbishment is needed, bring a builder to give you a rough idea of the costs. Visit any property you might consider on more than one occasion. See it, or at least the area, at different times of the day, at night and at the weekend.

Finally, do you like the house? Nothing can make you happy in a house you hate, no matter how great a bargain it is. There is no measure of a place to surpass basic gut feeling.

Further ideas on viewing property are outlined in Chapter 8, but do bear in mind that the priorities of someone buying rental property can differ significantly from those of someone buying their own home.

ALTERNATIVE SOURCES OF PROPERTY
Buying Privately

Occasionally, a seller decides to sell his property without the aid of an agent. Many people like to keep their affairs private and don't relish the thought of strangers – or worse, their neighbours – traipsing through their homes without any real interest in buying. Sometimes sellers want to keep their intentions private, even from their own families. Checking the classified ads in your local paper is often a good way to find properties which are not on the lists of the agents. Sometimes real bargains are to be found through word of mouth. Place an ad yourself in the '*Property Wanted*' column in your local paper. Don't forget the internet as a good source of off-the-books properties. Be aware, however, that, in buying privately, the balance of advantage lies with the seller who saves on fees by negotiating without an agent.

The process should be simpler than acting through an agent, since the middleman is out of the picture, but this is another of those ideas that works well in theory. People tend to forget that most agents are skilled negotiators. If a problem arises, it should be relatively straightforward to pick up the phone and iron it out with the seller on the spot. But the seller may not possess even basic negotiating skills, or worse, may not be trustworthy. When viewing a property without an agent be wary in your dealings and sensible about security. Bring someone with you when you go to view a property sourced from a newspaper or the internet.

Something else to watch out for is the seller who has placed his property on an agent's books then, dissatisfied with the progress of the sale, decides to have a go himself without bothering to inform the agent. I have come across situations where both the agent and the seller had accepted deposits on the same property. No purchaser in his right mind wants to get involved in that sort of mess, so *caveat emptor*.

Swapping Properties

This should be a great idea. If I own a property that you would like and you have a place that I want then it should be an easy matter to arrange a swap. The problem is that in the early nineties the government decided to impose stamp duty on both parties to such a deal. With increases in property prices, swapping has now become expensive. The exception is between close family members, e.g. parent and child, where no stamp duty applies. In these limited circumstances it can make excellent sense.

Buying Off the Plans

The trend towards buying new properties off the plans appears to be a growing one. The expensively produced, glossy brochures provided by most builders nowadays can be seductive, especially the photos of the cool kitchens with happy looking, beautiful people sitting down eating gourmet food. Come to think of it, that image is already dated. Recent brochures I've seen concentrate almost exclusively on the bedroom. Skip the photos and study the floor plans carefully. Take particular note of the room sizes. If you don't know much about measurements get out a tape or a ruler and measure out the distance in the room in which you are sitting. You might be surprised at how small some of the bedrooms, in particular, are in modern houses and apartments. Don't rely on what you see in the showhouse either. I once saw a showhouse with what must have been specially-commissioned smaller-than-normal beds. It wasn't at all obvious, but when I went back to the plans, sure enough the length of the room was only five foot ten, not long enough for a bed. To have placed the bed the other way would have meant putting it across either the doorway or the window! If you become skilled at reading plans you can save a lot of time looking at showhouses which you are not going to buy. But beware – floor plans are not always accurate.

The good news about buying directly off plans is that by the time the place is built it will almost certainly have appreciated considerably in value. On the other hand you are making an act of faith in the builder. Check around and do your best to ensure he is trustworthy. While many builders employ agents to do the selling for them, some, especially smaller companies, still deal directly with the customer. Generally builders won't negotiate on price as they have plenty of buyers. A useful, alternative tactic has always been to look for more for your money. The builder knows that it doesn't cost him that much to throw in a few extras while the workers are still on the site. Try, if you can, to avoid stage payments, a practice common outside Dublin whereby the purchaser ends up in the unenviable position of having paid about 90 per cent of the cost of the property, when only about 10 per cent of the work is done.

PRIVATE TREATY SALE

A private treaty sale refers to any sale other than an auction. Usually the sale is between two people who sign a contract of sale drawn up by the seller's solicitor. Sometimes, in an effort to minimise costs, it is suggested that both parties use the same solicitor. Do not be tempted by this suggestion as no solicitor can act impartially for both sides if a dispute arises.

Making an Offer

It is very important that you make the terms of your offer clear to the agent. For this reason I would recommend that an initial offer be made in writing. As speed is often of the essence – if you're very interested the chances are that others are too – the communication should be by fax or e-mail with a follow-up phone call to ensure that it has made its way to the right person. Before making your offer find out how long the property has been on the market and if any offers have already been made. An opening gambit might be in the region of 80–90 per cent of the asking price. Discuss this matter with the agent, but don't be pushed into making too high an initial offer.

Sealed Bids

If demand for a particular property is very high, something not uncommon in today's sellers' market, then the agent will sometimes recommend a system of sealed bids. This works rather like going to tender. The owner is not, however, obliged to accept the highest offer. Decide how much you are willing to pay and add on a few euro to give an odd amount such as €250,005. By doing so your offer might succeed over the nearest round figure.

Putting Down a Deposit

Whatever the method of sale, any offer you make on a property should be made subject to the following conditions where relevant:

- surveyor's report;
- availability of finance;
- contract; and
- good title.

Placing your deposit with the agent subject to these conditions allows you to exit from the deal without complications if you have sufficient cause. The amount you are offering should be clearly stated along with other factors that improve your buying position, such as mortgage approval or not having to sell another property. Being able to move quickly to complete the deal will endear you to the agent and the vendor and may mean that a lower offer from you will be accepted over a higher offer made by someone else.

Surveyor's Report

Some agents will not accept an offer until the purchaser has had a survey carried out on the property. While this might seem unfair to a purchaser who may eventually be outbid for the place, it does have the advantage of weeding out the property tourists who can often push up the price by making offers even though they are not in a position to buy.

The surveyor's report should be to your satisfaction. This does not of course mean that the property has to be perfect. Sometimes prospective purchasers are put off buying fine properties because of unrealistic reports. Remember that the surveyor's brief is to alert you to potential problems but some can be over zealous in their evaluation, failing to distinguish the relative importance of a cracked footpath to the rear and a serious crack in the wall indicating subsidence. So read the report with a sense of proportion. Some faults you can live with. Others, more serious, might quite correctly put you off buying the property.

Availability of Finance

Making your offer subject to finance means that if, for any unforeseen reason, your loan is not approved or some other, expected source of funds dries up, then you are not legally bound to proceed with the purchase. The benefits of this situation are immediately apparent when you consider the alternative, being obliged to proceed with the sale, or leaving yourself open to being sued for breach of contract.

Contract

The contract of sale, sets out clearly the terms of the sale and will be handled by both solicitors. Contracts must be signed by both parties in order for the agreement to be valid.

Good Title

A good title is usually straightforward for new properties as there are few complications. When it comes to older properties, however, perhaps the term *'Good Enough Title'* might be more apt. Houses, like people, tend to accumulate baggage with age. Obvious things like ensuring that the property genuinely belongs to the person who is selling it and that nobody else has a claim on it, form part of the checks the solicitor will carry out. A spouse, for example, does not have the right to sell a family home without the consent of the other partner. Difficulties can also arise in relation to things like rights of way over a property. Your solicitor will liaise with the lender on your behalf, as the mortgage becomes part of the deeds when the sale is completed.

Remember

Place a deposit on a property subject to:

- surveyor's report;
- availability of finance;
- contract; and
- good title.

THE ART OF THE DEAL

Having made an offer for the property you want to buy, the negotiations begin. The auctioneer will probably get back to you telling you of a larger offer from another buyer. In a sellers' market, as exists at the time of writing, it is common for a property to exceed the guide price as set by the agent. There are two unavoidable problems with the negotiation process. It is both time consuming and adversarial. If it goes on too long everybody gets short tempered. Every agent has had at least one sale fall through over some trivial issue which went on to-ing and fro-ing between the parties, to the point of exhaustion, neither side willing to compromise. Don't be afraid to ask the reason if your offer isn't accepted. The situation might not be irredeemable.

Unfortunately you are not yet out of the wood even if your offer *is* accepted. A nasty little thing called *'gazumping'* can stymie you now. This is a practice whereby the seller accepts a higher offer even though he or she has already accepted yours. Unfortunately it is quite legal as it is usually only when contracts have been signed by both parties that the agreement can be relied upon. (Gazumping should not be confused with *'gazundering'* (where do they get these words?) which involves the purchaser trying to renegotiate a lower price than that already agreed after he has seen off the opposition.)

Signing the Contract

You will, by now, have contacted your solicitor and asked him to act on your behalf in the purchase. The auctioneer will request a deposit of anything up to 5 per cent at this stage, but will often accept less.

When the booking deposit has been lodged with the agent, then the next step is for the agent to contact your solicitor and that of the vendor advising him of the terms of the deal. Your solicitor will then contact the vendor's solicitor and the contracts will be prepared. On signing the contract you must pay, usually, 10 per cent of the purchase price of the property. The original booking deposit, lodged with the agent, will form part of this amount. At this point it is essential to ensure that a list of all fixtures and fittings included in the sale is available. Study this list to be sure that it contains all of the agreed items. Generally if no list is available, the usual practice is that items attached to the walls of the building such as wall-mounted shelves, curtain rails and so on, should be left in the property.

The contract of sale will normally include an agreed closing date. That is the date when the balance of the money is paid over to the vendor and the purchaser receives the keys to his new home. The time lapse between signing the contract and completing the sale takes anything from four weeks to several months. As the purchaser, you are legally bound to fulfill all the terms of the contract or risk being sued by the vendor. At this point your solicitor may advise you to have the property insured. In most cases one of the conditions of the mortgage is that insurance on the property be maintained. It is in your own best interest to be covered from the time you sign the contract, whether or not you have a mortgage.

On completion of the sale and receipt of the keys you will be required to pay stamp duty on the property where it is applicable. In Ireland stamp duty is very high, up to 9 per cent (see Appendix 1). It is hard to believe but, when the total tax take on a newly built house is calculated the figure is a whopping 37–39 per cent of the price! Your solicitor's last job, apart from sending you his bill, is to register your deeds with the Land Registry Office.

BUYING AT AUCTION

According to the IAVI, one of the auctioneers' professional associations, about 10 per cent of properties sold in Ireland each year are auctioned. Auctions are not for the lily-livered, but for those intrepid souls who know what they are about and who are disciplined enough not to get carried away in the heat of the moment.

Unlike other forms of sale, buying at auction means that every detail must be sorted out beforehand. The most important thing to know about auctions is that you commit yourself absolutely, on the day, to buying the property. As an indication of commitment you must pay 10 per cent of the price on the spot and you can expect to forfeit this deposit if you fail to complete the purchase. In addition, you could be held liable for all costs associated with the auction and even for the difference should the property be sold subsequently at a lower price. It is a good idea to attend a few other auctions in advance of the one you are interested in so that you know what to expect.

As for any other type of sale, visit the property a few times and familiarise yourself with the area. (See the section on viewing a property.) All surveys must be carried out in advance. Decide on the maximum amount that you are prepared to pay, taking the auctioneer's guide price into account and have all of the details of your mortgage ironed out. It would be extremely foolish to commit yourself to buying a property if your loan sanction is not copper-fastened in advance. Arrange for your solicitor to view the title deeds beforehand and make any searches he deems necessary in order to ensure that there are no nasty surprises. This should be done as far in advance as possible so that he has sufficient time to advise you properly. Remember you are not his only client.

On the day of the auction you should arrive early in the company of your solicitor. Most auctions are held in the auctioneer's office, but if it is a high-profile event and a large crowd is expected, it is usually held in a nearby hotel. It's a good idea to ring the auctioneer in advance to make sure that the property has not been withdrawn or sold prior to auction. On that point, it's worth a try to enquire whether *you* could buy beforehand but don't offer your maximum figure. You should also find out if the guide price has changed in the course of the advertising campaign. It sometimes does so in response to the level of interest shown. Register as a bidder when you arrive. Check you have the required 10 per cent deposit with you, either in cash or banker's draft. Ask the auctioneer in advance what is acceptable.

The proceedings will begin with the reading of the conditions of sale. This is a legal requirement. Boring it may be, but don't allow your eyes to glaze over, they are important. Don't make the first bid if you can avoid it as by doing so you could cause the bidding to start higher than it might otherwise.

The advantage of an auction is the avoidance of long drawn-out negotiations. The downside is that there can be only one successful bidder. Underbidders have to grin and bear their legal and valuation costs, perhaps many times. If you are successful, however, be prepared to hand over the required deposit immediately and to close the sale within the required time limit. You must also insure the property without delay.

If the property fails to reach the reserve set by the owner, the auctioneer may decide to withdraw it from the sale. Should this occur then leave your name and address with the auctioneer because the seller may accept less after an unsuccessful auction.

Congratulations
You're ready to move in!
If you've got this far it's time to crack open the champagne and enjoy your new home.

Chapter 6
Building it Yourself

Few things in life have as much potential to deliver satisfaction and pride as building your own home. Unfortunately there are also few things more likely to shorten your life span if it goes wrong. Every year hundreds of one-off homes are built throughout the country. Within the constraints of planning permission and building regulations, as a self-builder you have the unique opportunity to create a truly inspirational living space. Your vision can be as exciting as your imagination and your budget will allow. New materials and fresh ways of looking at space and light open up new architectural possibilities. Features such as double height rooms, walls of glass, sleeping lofts, vaulted ceilings and galleries are all possible. Modern plumbing and technology provide even more choices. Clean, efficient, heating, including underfloor systems where there are no unsightly radiators, air conditioning and those stylish, Spanish and Italian bathroom suites create beautiful, easily maintained, energy-saving homes. If you decide to take the self-build route, it may be the only time in your life when you have the freedom to create, from start to finish, your very own living environment for yourself and your family. You can have rooms that are just the right size and flooring, kitchen, bathroom, lighting and colour schemes all exactly how you want them.

FINDING A SITE

Contrary to popular belief, there is no shortage of sites on which to build your house in rural Ireland. Drive a short distance out from any town or suburbs in any direction and you won't find any lack of space. Fields stretch as far as the eye can see in all directions. The problem is finding a site on which permission to build will be granted by the local authority. Most of us who have any connection with the countryside have heard a myriad stories of young people, whose ancestors have been living in an area for generations, being refused permission to build. Not only that, but you will be told, with knowing looks, about the rich and well-connected who have no problem getting planning permission. However, the statistics would seem to belie the accepted truth in this case.

A recent investigation carried out by the Department of the Environment, Housing & Local Government found that of the areas sampled, an average of 75 per cent of planning applications for single, one-off, rural houses were granted. Where permission was refused the reasons given generally related to issues of land use, traffic safety, public health or protection of the natural and cultural heritage.

Planners are keen to promote small, village-type developments of 10 to 15 houses. In a move to free up more sites for building, however, the government, perhaps in response to pressure from certain rural development groups, recently issued *The Sustainable Rural Housing Guidelines*. Under these guidelines 250,000 new, one-off, houses, will be granted planning permission in rural areas over the next 20 years.

One might question the wisdom of such a course in terms of the common good. I wonder if the implications of a major increase in the numbers of stand-alone houses in the countryside have been adequately studied. The measure should, on the other hand, give grounds for optimism to those who want to build in their native place. In city areas too, on foot of changes in the building density levels allowed, it should be easier to get that elusive planning permission. Bigger, older, detached houses often have large gardens, very much in demand as plots on which to build. A trend has lately emerged in more expensive areas, where an older house, whatever its condition, is demolished to make way for a new, which often contains several units, either houses or apartments. The last frontier in the great building surge is the area just outside the suburbs in our cities which is usually zoned commercial or green belt. Can these areas hold out for long against the ubiquitous urban sprawl?

Apart from the obvious attractions of the countryside, such as tranquility and community life, people often value their roots and passionately want to stay in their own area. Some are fortunate enough to acquire a site from a family member, thereby greatly reducing the cost of their home. If you are not so lucky and you are in the market for a site on a limited budget, then the first thing is to avoid the high-profile, trendy areas where the prices are like Lotto numbers. There are still genuine bargains to be had in lovely, out of the way places, not yet discovered by the masses. With persistence and a little luck such places can still be found, often surprisingly close to cities and towns. Go to your local planning office where you will find the staff very helpful and check any area you are considering for restrictive zoning which might prohibit residential development. Many variations in policy exist regarding how individual county councils regulate planning. Some, especially those near Dublin – Wicklow, Meath and Louth for example – are highly restrictive. Some demand that the applicant be a long-term resident of the county while others insist on family ties and employment in the area. Even individual planners vary in their attitude and interpretation of policy. Areas of the country where there is less demand for planning permission are much less restrictive.

When buying a site always buy subject to planning permission and you won't go far wrong. If things don't work out you can then walk away having lost only the cost of the planning application. Failure to do so can leave you with a useless, though expensive, plot of ground. Don't forget low-cost housing sites which are sometimes available from local authorities if your budget is low (see Chapter 3).

Remember
If you are buying a site be sure to buy subject to planning permission.

WHAT TO LOOK FOR
If you studied Irish in school you may have come across a book called *Seadhna*. '*Tig beag deas cluthar, ag bun chnoic, ar thaobh na fothana*'

was the description of Seadhna's house, which roughly translated means '*a nice, small, cosy house at the bottom of the sheltered side of a hill*'. This description quite accurately reflects building practice in Ireland up to about 40 or 50 years ago. I would no more suggest that we all live in little cottages than I would that we become a nation of shepherds, but I do think our forefathers had the right idea. A house like Seadhna's with its natural shelter from rain and wind will keep you warmer in winter, cooler in summer, save you money on heating and be kinder to the environment than many modern homes.

Price and availability will govern your choice of site, but it really is worthwhile, both for the sake of your enjoyment of your home and its resale value, to take environmental factors into account. Think calm and tranquil rather than aggressive domination of the landscape and keep some of the following points in mind.

- Try not to build in a prominent location such as the brow of a hill where the house will look like something that has fallen from the sky rather than a part of the landscape.
- Do not build in an exposed area which is subject to harsh weather in winter.
- In a rural area a private water supply and waste disposal unit will probably be necessary so watch out for rocky or boggy sites unsuitable for the septic tank. On a difficult or restricted site there is, however, the possibility of installing a chemical treatment unit.
- There are strict rules about how far the water source and the septic tank must be from the house and from each other. The site must, at least, be large enough to accommodate all three and have them sufficiently far enough away from those of neighbouring houses.
- In general, the scale of the house should match the size of the site, a larger house on a bigger site and vice versa.
- Trees and shrubs, either existing or newly planted, can be used for shelter and privacy. In a rural area these should be native species such as beech and ash.
- Orientation is important. Try to get a site where the house can be built with the main living rooms facing south for light and warmth.
- Though you will be governed by what the planners deem

acceptable, the site should, ideally, have enough scope for the house to be set back from the road and at an angle to it.

- Much of the charm of the countryside is in the trees, natural hedgerows, ditches and stone walls that abound, so consider yourself lucky if you can find a site which incorporates some of these features and retain them as far as possible.

Following these guidelines should result in a well-situated house.

Remember
Gently does it. Go for harmony with your surroundings, not domination.

WHAT TO BUILD AND HOW TO BUILD IT
Having acquired your site, the next stop is to consider what you want to build on it. You have several choices.

Employ a Building Contractor
This is the usual procedure when buying a newly built house in a suburban estate. For a one-off house the builder would, typically, be a small, local building firm. Once your plans have been drawn up and approved by the local authority planning office, you could contract out the entire job. This might be your best option if you want a minimum of involvement with the process. This level of convenience does not, of course, come cheaply.

Build Using a Package Supplier
There are several companies on the market which supply plans and all of the materials needed for a standard house. Most companies will deal with the planners and erect the structure according to their own plans. This option can be price-competitive as the houses are designed to maximise the amount of space for the price, but such designs often lack any unique features and tend to be sold on a one-size-fits-all basis. Problems with planning often arise as a result. Standardised houses with no consideration for the site or its environs are usually frowned on by the planners.

Build by DIY
This involves laying block on block yourself and roping in all of your relatives and friends who have useful skills to contribute. I know families, one in particular comes to mind, that are fortunate to have a number of tradespeople among them. They have combined forces, successfully, to build a house for each member in turn, supplying labour as required and hiring outside expertise only when necessary. This is by far the cheapest option but, unless you are willing to give up the day job to manage the project, or you don't mind waiting for years to see your house finished, then forget it. Also, do not be tempted to do specialised jobs like electrical work yourself. The Electricity Supply Board will not connect your house unless a competent, certified, electrician has carried out the electrical installation.

Build Your House by Direct Labour
This means employing tradespeople individually or in groups to carry out each section of the work. It is the preferred option of many as it is cheaper than employing a building firm. Project management is the key to getting it right. Architects and engineers usually offer such a service for about 3–5 per cent of the cost of the work. Alternatively, you may decide that you have sufficient experience to do it yourself. You may have, but the aim is to bring the house to completion on time and on budget. There is too much at stake for self-indulgence or fantasy. You need to know what you are doing and then consider, realistically, how much time you have at your disposal to spend supervising the work.

ENGINEERS, ARCHITECTS AND QUANTITY SURVEYORS
The Engineer
Usually the first person on the job, the engineer marks out the boundaries of the site and draws it on the Ordnance Survey map of the area. He will also produce a site-plan, positioning the house, septic tank water source and putting in any pre-existing features on the site. It is essential that this work be carried out by a competent profess-ional, otherwise your project could end up as a bureaucratic nightmare when you get to the planning stage.

The Architect
The architect's job is to design your house and produce a set of drawings in accordance with your needs, the Local Authority

Planning Guidelines and the building regulations. Consultation is vital in this process. It is your expectations, how you see yourself living in the house, which will determine the shape and use of space in the final structure. But do allow yourself to be guided. Why keep a dog and bark yourself?

Architects can be expensive and this work can often be adequately done by an engineer or a draughtsman. You can even buy ready-made plans off the internet or copy them from a book. But a good architect can lift your house from the mundane and transform it into something special. He can often save you money in the process through clever use of materials and there is no doubt that he can add thousands to the resale value. More importantly, living with good design can actually make a difference to how restful and happy you feel in your home when it is finished, something impossible to quantify in monetary terms.

The Quantity Surveyor

A detailed specification for the works based on the architect's drawings, an estimate of the costs and schedule of work and payments to the builders are all part of the job of the quantity surveyor. The need for such detailed planning is obvious on large projects. On a smaller job, such as a single house, it may not be the usual practice. If, however, you are considering building by direct labour, rather than engaging a building contractor, then employing a quantity surveyor is probably a good idea. This function may of course be carried out by your architect or engineer. Once again, discuss fees and level of service in advance.

Be sure at all times that you are dealing with qualified professionals. There is no law to stop anybody setting up as an architect, or engineer, without any qualifications whatsoever and there are many chancers out there. Finally, negotiate fees and the level of service you need in advance. See also 'Some Elements of Good Design' on page 78.

YOUR BUILDER

If you haven't built before and have no idea of what is involved, you would be well advised to hand the project over to a builder. A good building contractor will handle the entire job, organising everything form start to finish. All you will have to do, unless something goes wrong, is turn up occasionally in the evenings to see how the job is progressing. You will also have the nicer parts of the project to look after like picking out items such as kitchen units, fireplaces and paint colours. Be warned, however, that this is not a cheap option. Such convenience can cost. There is one cost advantage in employing a builder, however. If you buy building materials yourself you will pay 21 per cent VAT on everything, a builder buying the same materials however will pay only 13.5 per cent.

When you have a builder in mind try to get a personal recommendation from someone you know who has already employed him. If this proves difficult ask him for references from a few former clients. Most people are happy to recommend someone who has done a good job for them. Ask him for phone numbers and ring them yourself.

Having received three quotations for the job, you must make sure that they are comparable with each other. Even though builders work from the architect's drawings when compiling their estimates and quotations, some will include the cost of items such as tiling and painting while others will not. Be absolutely clear on the question of materials. Clarify exactly who will pay for what, and then you will be ready to compare the differing prices. Don't base your final choice of builder on price alone. Building a house is a major undertaking likely to cause a lot of stress. It should, without doubt, carry a government health warning. Do yourself a favour and pick a builder who is easy to work with and then cross all of your fingers and toes and pray for guidance! Taking on a builder is always a leap in the dark. You need all the help you can get.

USING DIRECT LABOUR

Using direct labour may take a great deal of time and organisation and is definitely not for the faint-hearted or the novice, though it is a way to save a lot of money. Not only is it cheaper but, all going well, your level of satisfaction with a job well done will be higher than if you had used a builder. The easiest procedure when employing direct labour is to break down the complete project into its component parts before you begin and get at least one separate quotation for each phase of the job (and ideally two or even three). Use only tradespeople you know personally and trust, or who come recommended by someone you know. As with a builder, clarify the exact position regarding materials, what will be supplied and what you will pay for.

Have a clear schedule made out before you begin. You may not stick to it exactly, but at least you will have all of the elements of the job on paper.

In many instances a tradesman will need to visit the site on more than one occasion. The electrician, for example, will do a *'first fix'*, when installing the main wiring system and a *'second fix'* when the plastering is completed, putting in switches and sockets. He may need to return again when the decorating is finished to install things like light fittings.

The first time I got involved in a building project I was surprised to find that on-site co-operation was very good. As a result the whole job was far less complicated than I had anticipated. Tradespeople are generally used to working together on building sites. They exchanged phone numbers without any interference from me and got on with the job, connecting with each other as the need arose.

Try to keep in mind a few golden rules for building by direct labour.

- *Never* pay for a job until it is fully finished.
- If extras are required, get a separate quotation for them *before* the work begins.
- Understand the difference between a quotation and an estimate. One should be an exact calculation, the other is only a good guess. This is vital.
- Your architect or engineer should be involved with the whole building process in a supervisory capacity to ensure planning recommendations and building regulations are adhered to. This is not mere nit-picking. When you come to sell the property your purchaser will find it difficult to get a mortgage on a property which is not fully compliant with all requirements.
- Electricians must have RECI certification.
- Plumbers must be registered with Bord Gáis if they are to install gas heating.
- Building contractors are responsible for insuring their workers. You have to consider the consequences of someone being injured on your site. Only people with a valid safety pass should be allowed on site while work is going on. Luckily, there is now a comprehensive insurance package, tailor-made for

self-builders. In addition to employers' liability, it covers theft of materials from the site and most other potential disasters. Ask your broker about this.

Remember
Never confuse an estimate and a quotation.

FINANCE

The rules on income, deposits and credit history outlined in Chapter 2 apply equally to the self-builder. Most mortgage brokers and financial institutions will be happy to discuss your precise needs when self-building and tailor a mortgage accordingly. Don't forget to budget for somewhere to live while your home is under construction. You are very fortunate if you have relatives or friends willing to put you up for the duration. A low-cost alternative to paying rent is to put a mobile home on the site after you have put in the services. It may not be the last word in luxury, but the discomfort can be outweighed by the convenience of being on hand to make sure all is going according to plan.

Your quantity surveyor, having examined your plans, will be in a position to cost the project with a good degree of accuracy.

BUILDING STANDARDS

The standard of finish that you want will have a huge bearing on the bottom line. There are roughly three grades of finish.

Basic

This includes standard timber joinery, internal stud partitions, a basic, off-the-peg kitchen and bottom-of-the-range sanitary ware in the bathroom. Happily, builders of housing estates have moved beyond this rock-bottom standard to satisfy their now more discerning customers. More stringent building regulations introduced in recent years, which make items such as double glazing and insulation mandatory, have also played their part in improving standards.

Superior

This standard of finish has now virtually become the norm. It encompasses pvc or hardwood, double-glazed windows and doors, internal block walls, made-to-measure kitchens, good-quality sanitary ware, some tiling, paths outside and usually some attempt to plant grass in the front garden.

Luxury

This term, though now almost meaningless due to overuse, should mean best quality finishes throughout. Bespoke, solid wood kitchens and wardrobes, wooden floors, top quality sanitary ware, tiling and maybe underfloor heating may be expected. It is in the area of design, however, that a luxury finish stands out from the rest.

INSURANCE

As already mentioned, building contractors are responsible for insuring their workers and to make sure they do so you should always see the policy covering workers on your site. This is necessary to indemnify you in the event of an accident. As the owner of the site where work is going on, you have to consider your legal liabilities. As soon as you sign a contract to purchase your site you should, without delay, put insurance in place which covers all aspects of building. This is available through your broker.

THE PLANNING PROCESS

A grant of planning permission, despite what many people think, is not a purely arbitrary decision made by the planning official according to which side of the bed he happened to get out of that morning. Local authorities have development plans, renewed every five years, which outline the general development objectives in each local area within their ambit. This plan is adopted by the council only after extensive consultation with community groups and members of the public. If you're not happy with the direction that planning in your area is taking don't blame the planners – get active and involved and make sure that your voice is heard the next time that the plan is up for review. As well as the zoning of different areas – residential, commercial, agricultural, etc. – the requirements for planning permission are outlined in some detail in the Development Plan. Acceptable finishes for the walls of buildings, permissible roof heights and other restrictions, many of which will impact on the design of you house are included. This is why you would be well advised to meet the planning official for the area for pre-planning discussions on what would be acceptable on your particular site. Many people employ an architect or engineer to complete the planning application on their behalf. This is necessary as the drawings and other documents required include technical specifications beyond the capabilities of most non-professionals. Be very careful whom you employ to do this work. When people feel out of their depth, they may take a step back from the process once the professionals become involved. This could be a mistake. There are many so-called professionals, who waste a great deal of their clients' time and money by submitting slipshod and incomplete applications then blame the planners when things go wrong. Check all submissions yourself.

Outline Planning Permission
In order to discover whether or not, in principle, you will be allowed build on your chosen site, it may be a good idea to apply for outline planning permission (OPP). The advantage of this course is that the not inconsiderable cost of applying for Full Planning Permission (FPP) will not be wasted on a lost cause, as only minimal drawings are required. Outline Planning Permission remains valid for three years and it should go without saying that work may not begin on a site until FPP has been granted.

Full Planning Permission
With luck, FPP should take no longer than two to three months, though it could take a lot longer if there are objections from third parties. You must, at any rate, get a response, even if it is only an acknowledgment within that time or be granted permission by default. Though many applications will require that you submit extra information, or modify some features of your design, all of the standard documentation should be submitted at the outset. The following documents are required.

- An extract from the Ordnance Survey map of the area (six copies) showing all significant features of the location. The boundaries of the site should be clearly marked out on this map.
- The site layout (six copies) showing where the house, water source, septic tank and any other buildings will be placed.
- Plans, elevations and sections of the proposed building (six copies).

- A copy of the public notice from the newspaper – be sure to include the whole page, not just the advertisement, in order to verify the date on which the notice appeared.
- A copy of the site notice and an indication of where on the site it is positioned. It is a legal requirement that a notice outlining the proposed development should be posted on the site. A template is available from your local authority with spaces on it where you can fill in your own details.
- If necessary, a certificate should be included stating that compliance with Part V of the Planning and Development Act 2000 does not apply (this relates to special areas of conservation, listed buildings, etc.).
- Where the site does not front on to the public road, a letter from your solicitor is required stating that you have right of way access.
- Copies of any objections lodged.
- Evidence of arrangements to move electricity and telephone poles where necessary.
- A schedule of all the documents submitted.
- The appropriate fee should also be included.

The above list is not exhaustive, but is fairly typical of what is required, and the planning authority may seek additional documentation. It is a good idea to arrange a consultation before lodging your application as any extras may then be supplied immediately. This could prevent delays later in the process. If planning permission is not granted, or if the conditions imposed appear too restrictive, then there is provision for appeal to An Bord Pleanála. Appeals must be made within one month of the decision. Third parties may also make an appeal within this time frame.

SOME ELEMENTS OF GOOD DESIGN

Have you every noticed how many modern houses in the countryside look slightly startled. It is as if they were surprised to find themselves in such surroundings when they were supposed to be somewhere else, in the suburbs perhaps? This does not mean that we cannot successfully build in a modern style in a rural location. There is no onus on anybody to continually replicate older forms. Such a course, far from being desirable, would leave us with little but pastiche – fake old – like those awful Olde Worlde pubs. Good design should show a respect for tradition and also produce something innovative and exciting.

If, in your choice of site, you have given some thought to how your house will blend in with its surroundings, then you will want to follow this through with equal sensitivity when attending to the design. The aim, once again, is to achieve harmony between the building and its environment. Ultimately, this is what will work best, giving your home that elusive x factor (as opposed to the *Wow* factor, which is something else entirely). I really do believe, and research backs this up, that good design can make people happier in their homes and workplaces. Think of the home you are setting up as a quiet reflection of your personality rather that an aggressive attempt to stamp your presence on the landscape. Take time to consider the situation of the house. Try to be aware of traditional building designs in the area and to be respectful towards them. A good architect can take many different elements into account in his work.

For a really first rate treatment of these matters read *Cork Rural Design Guide* (produced by Cork County Council). It should be mandatory reading for self-builders everywhere in Ireland. A number of characteristics worth developing are suggested. While these are intended as guidelines for the Cork area, they could act as a yardstick of good design in virtually any rural area. They include:

- simplicity;
- good proportions;
- a satisfactory balance between the area of wall and of door and window openings;
- good-quality materials; and
- an absence of stuck-on bits and frills.

Final points to consider are proportion and scale. Add-ons such as conservatories, should be built in proportion to the original structure and should not dwarf it. Also, the shape should mirror the original house. Dormers and roof lights, where used, should not be so big that they dominate the front aspect of the house. Most importantly, emphasising harmony once again, all materials and finishes used should be consistent with other buildings locally rather than standing out like the proverbial *'sore thumb'*.

Having your house designed with these principles in mind will not only ensure a vastly better house which has a greater resale value, but your chances of getting planning permission immediately are greatly improved, saving you time, money and stress.

Case Study

Jennifer and Brian were tired of living in flats. They had lived together for five years and their dream of having a home of their own seemed to be disappearing in the wake of price rises. They were saving, as much as they could without giving up all pretensions to a social life, but prices were going up faster than they could save. Jennifer had her mind made up on one issue – there was absolutely no way she was going to become pregnant until they had their own place. She felt out of place and isolated enough in the city without having a baby where no family support or help would be available. What could they do? Their situation appeared hopeless.

However about a year later, a solution presented itself in an unexpected way. Brian's Uncle Martin had lived all his life in Wexford near where Brian had grown up. After his sudden death it was discovered that he had left a plot of land to each of his nieces and nephews. Jennifer and Brian immediately saw this as the solution to their difficulties. They found that when the cost of the site was taken care of, building a house was a feasible proposition. Their first call was to a mortgage broker who gave them an immediate customised quote for a mortgage which was realistic and manageable. They bought a caravan and installed it on the site. Though cramped, living there meant they saved a substantial amount on rent, money which was very welcome for floors and furniture.

Brian had worked on building sites with a local builder as a student so he had a good idea of the processes involved in building a house. They were fortunate that Brian's brother is an electrician and Jennifer has a cousin who is a plasterer. They were reliable and were willing to help supervise the project as well as donating their skills on the construction. An architect was commissioned to produce a design as they wanted to make the most of their sea view. Jennifer's dad thought this an unwarranted expense, but they stuck to their guns. The result was, they felt, well worth it. Big windows made the whole place bright and airy. Clever use of different levels gave a wonderful feeling of lightness and space. For the exterior, considering stone beyond their budget, they decided on a paint finish. The architect's choice of colours was soft green and grey.

Unlike some people, they found that their planning permission was granted with a minimum of delay and bother. This they put down to the fact that, since they were surrounded by family members, there were no third parties to object and to the quality of the design submitted by their architect.

So for everything has gone remarkable smoothly. They expect to be moving in before Christmas and guess what! Their baby is due in the spring.

Jennifer and Brian's story involves quite a lot of luck. Not everyone can expect to be so fortunate. But there is also much hard work, saving and flexibility in their story. Without their determination they would not have been in a position to benefit from the good fortune which came their way.

Section Two
Residential Investment

Chapter 7

The Landlord

WHY BUY TO LET?

Bricks and mortar is the investment of choice of a great many Irish people. Paper wealth has little attraction for us – we like to be able to see, touch and feel our riches. As a nation we have never taken to stocks and shares as many ordinary people have in the US. Our one mass foray into that market, when we queued to buy our allocation of Telecom Éireann shares, complaining only that we couldn't get more and believing we couldn't lose, has left a bitter aftertaste. On the other hand, seeing the value of our homes reach into the stratosphere in the last decade was something we could enjoy without any obvious risk. Wide-eyed in amazement, we looked at the comparisons made in newspapers between Irish house prices and those around the globe. We were delighted and appalled in equal measure to find that a modest cottage in one of the more prestigious areas of Dublin (like Dalkey or Foxrock) could cost as much as a small château in France or a condominium in Hollywood.

CAPITAL APPRECIATION

Arguments made for investing in your own home can similarly be made for buy-to-let properties, namely capital appreciation and ease of finance. Factor in rent, and you also have a very well-paid part-time job. As most of us think the area of commercial property is complicated and best left to the professionals, we have been attracted to the idea of buying houses and apartments as an investment. In the past 10 years property has out-performed almost all other investments. Low or even negative stock-market returns and abysmal interest on deposits have combined to make good old bricks and mortar the small investors' choice.

When worthwhile opportunities are limited for most people and, with a considerable amount of '*Celtic Tiger*' cash still about, property prices may well continue the upward path which has characterised the last few years, although at a slower pace. Against this argument is the fact that last year a record number of new housing units was built in this state. For the first time supply and demand were roughly equal and in 2004 the building boom continued. Inevitably some of the heat will go from the property market, though most experts agree that a price crash is unlikely. For many, especially the self-employed, property has become their pension plan and they are now breathing a sigh of relief that they chose property over shares. I know many landlords who currently hold a large number of properties and are still adding to their portfolios, undeterred by rising prices, or fear of a market crash.

> **Remember**
> €300,000 invested in a bank for one year will, at the time of writing, yield about €1,455 after deduction of DIRT tax.
>
> €300,000 invested in property will yield, on average, €21,000 in capital appreciation @ 7% p.a. and approximately €12,000 in rent, a total of €33,000.

RENTAL INCOME

Capital appreciation is only half the story. There is another reason to invest in house property – and that's rent. There is always a demand for rented housing. In Ireland we have one of the lowest number of households per head of population in the developed world. Also, our population is expanding significantly due to natural growth and immigration. What this means is that, if we follow social trends established in the US and other European countries, in the future more people will live in smaller groups or alone, thus increasing the number of households. Currently in New York City a staggering 80 per cent of people live alone. This must cause us to pause for thought and reconsider our cherished notions of traditional family life as being the norm.

Undoubtedly some landlords, seeing the large numbers of new houses and apartment blocks being built in almost every town and village in the country, are worried about oversupply. But those of us who have been in the business for many years know that the market is continually adjusting. There have always been challenges: new standards imposed by the local authorities, a registration scheme introduced in the mid-nineties, changing rules on Mortgage Interest Tax Relief on foot of the Bacon reports, the list is endless. But after a while the dust always settles, if only for short while. Inflation carries on and in a few years the sum initially invested will probably seem small in comparison to the then current prices. At the end of 2004 an air of optimism about the Irish economy and a surprising level of population growth brought good news to the property market.

FINANCE
Low interest rates and the ready availability of buy-to-let mortgages have made buying a second house or apartment a feasible option for many who in the past would never have aspired to owning more than their own home. Without specialised knowledge or expertise, it would be difficult for an ordinary person who does not have large amounts of capital at his disposal to become involved in many areas of investment. In addition, most people are familiar with the private rental sector having come into contact with it at some time in their lives, either as tenants when they are young, as parents of a college-going son or daughter or indirectly through friends. When funds are available (perhaps through inheritance or a large redundancy package) and a mortgage can be arranged relatively easily, it would appear to be a sensible option to buy a property and let it out.

WHO ARE THE LANDLORDS?
Is there a '*typical*' landlord? The vast majority of landlords in this country are comfortably off, though not vastly wealthy, and have one or two reasonably well-furnished and maintained houses or apartments. They are people looking for a safe haven for a little spare cash, people who like the idea of a sideline, which supplements

their income and provides them with a nest egg for that '*rainy day*'. There are some who set out to be landlords but many others fall into being property investors almost in spite of themselves. Seldom do they decide to give up the day job and become full-time professionals in the business though some do eventually expand their portfolios sufficiently to make a comfortable living from their rental incomes. By devoting their energies to managing their properties and keeping an eye on the market, these part-timers can do very well indeed. Below are some of the types of people who fall into this category.

Inheritors of Property

It is likely that the majority of small landlords, those with just one house to let, are inheritors of a family home. Many never considered becoming landlords prior to their inheritance and don't go on to develop their interest by acquiring further properties. However, they are shrewd enough to see property as a solid investment and to benefit from the extra cash the rental income brings.

Those Without a Pension

A great number of PAYE workers do not have adequate pension provision (or any pension provision) for their retirement. In their twenties and thirties they don't see this as an issue, especially since these are often expensive years when people are setting up home and starting families. Buying a property to let is often the preferred option for a secure future for those in their forties and fifties as buying a private pension can be prohibitively costly if it is started late. Recognising this, in an effort to help people who are without a pension, the government has made generous tax concessions available for those who take out a pension mortgage. Your mortgage broker will outline the scheme to you as it applies in your particular circumstances.

Changes announced in the 2004 Finance Act mean that those who have invested in Self-Direct Trusts may now borrow on the strength of these funds. This gives holders a much greater scope for property investment. (See also Chapter 9.)

People Seeking a Supplementary Retirement Income

Financial advisers, independent ones, *not* those whose job it is to sell insurance policies of various kinds, often recommend that clients buy property with their retirement gratuity especially if the amount of their pension is small. This option can be very useful in increasing income and has the advantage that rent is more or less linked to inflation unlike most pensions. Many people have peace of mind knowing that they can release capital in the future to fund lifestyle changes, such as living in a retirement home.

Disappointed Pension Holders
Many people have been disappointed that their pension funds did not perform as well as they believed they would. From the late nineties pension performance has been so poor and charges on policies so high that some are now worth less than the sums invested to begin with.

Temporary and Reluctant Landlords
Landlords are as diverse a group of people as you could imagine. They have various reasons to let rather then sell property they are not living in. People who move to another city or even abroad, perhaps to take up alternative employment, often rent out their homes while they decide if the move is to be permanent.

Another group comprises older people in need of nursing home care. The family, not wishing to sell their older relative's home for sentimental reasons, often rent it out to defray the high cost of this care.

Some defer selling their houses, letting them instead, perhaps in anticipation of price rises or because of temporary difficulties such as road works which might adversely affect the price.

Parents of Third-Level Students
It often makes good sense for parents to buy a house or apartment for their children to use while they are in college. This applies particularly when there is more then one child involved as the cost of renting accommodation can be very high. Often renting one or more spare rooms to another student can partially, or even wholly, offset the costs. Some parents set up trusts in favour of their children. This is a tax-efficient way of providing them with student accommodation. Your solicitor will advise you about this procedure. When the children are finished college, the house often continues to be let, thus the parents become landlords almost by default.

High Earners Seeking Tax-Efficient Investment

A number of schemes exist whereby taxpayers can benefit from allowances on their capital outlay when buying property in certain designated areas. By investing in these schemes, either purely as an investor or as an owner-occupier, those on high incomes and in the higher tax bracket can dramatically reduce their tax bill.

Both landlords and tenants used to have a very negative image. Remember *Rising Damp* which featured Leonard Rossiter as Rigsby, a seedy, money-grabbing, greasy character who presided over a dingy, rundown hovel. He is meant to portray the typical landlord, a tightfisted scrooge dealing with tenants from the ranks of the sad, the bad and the mad. It worked at the time because, like all comedy, it contained just a grain of perceived truth. I like to think it wouldn't mean much to today's younger generation.

Here in Ireland even the word '*landlord*' has unfortunate historical associations and will be forever linked in our consciousness with other words like '*rackrent*', '*bailiffs*' and '*boycott*'. As a result, we have missed out on a long and comfortable tradition of renting property that exists in other countries. In Scottish cities for example, there have always been tenements, a term with quite a different meaning to that given it here. In Scotland the word applies to any building laid out in apartments or flats. In London too, a city which was the epitome of architectural excellence and elegance at the beginning of the twentieth century, over 90 per cent of residences were rented privately from their owners. In Dublin, by contrast, we think of the poverty of the slums when we think of the rental market of former times. Think of Sean O'Casey and his cast of characters who maintained their dignity against the odds, given the terrible condition of their surroundings. It would of course be naïve to suggest that slums were confined to Dublin. All cities had their dark undersides where poverty and degredation were the norm, often, it must be admitted, presided over by exploitative landlords.

More recently, people who rented their homes, either from their local authorities or through the private sector, were stigmatised and often given a tough time by neighbours who thought them inferior. In the twenty-first century such images are outmoded. They have nothing to do with modern landlord and tenant relationships.

> **Remember**
> Many landlords begin reluctantly and go on to find that they
> enjoy it and become very successful.

WHO ARE THE TENANTS?

In the twentieth-first century tenants are not always people who
cannot afford their own homes. Nowadays mobility is a huge factor in
how we live our lives. More and more, long-term renting is becoming
a choice for people who are young and need flexibility. Many are
unwilling to saddle themselves with a 25–30-year mortgage.
Employment contracts are becoming shorter, six months to a year
now being commonplace. For people in this position short-term
renting is the only viable option. Renting is, however, not confined to
the young. With the rise in the rate of marriage breakups a steady
stream of middle-aged people, mostly men, has emerged to be a
sizeable sector of the rental market. It would appear that we are, over
time, albeit very slowly, coming closer to the situation pertaining in
mainland Europe where renting is the norm.

Tenants Fall into Six Main Categories

Students

Rental returns are good in this sector of the market, but this is
balanced out by having the property vacant over the summer months.
Also, due to tax incentives available to investors in newly built student
accommodation, the traditional student houses and flats are reported
to be less popular with students than before.

Young Professionals

These are singles or couples who often have high disposable incomes
and can demand high-quality accommodation. Usually they are good
tenants though they can be demanding, expecting a high level of
service and prompt attention when things go wrong.

Families

A family with children may be trading up and require temporary
accommodation between selling one home and moving into another
or the parents might be working in the area on a temporary contract.

They can often be excellent tenants to deal with. Children can, of course, cause extra wear and tear, but this is usually offset by the extra care families take not to do any real damage. Family lettings tend to be either short-term, three to six months for people between homes, or more or less permanent as long-term tenants become embedded in an area. Up to now most families who rented long-term were local authority tenants.

Divorced and Separated People
This is a growing sector of the market as the divorce rate increases in this country. It is largely confined to men.

Corporate Letting
The main advantage of corporate letting, where a company is the tenant rather than an individual, is security. There is no need to check the individual tenants. Blue-chip companies expect high-quality accommodation, furnishing and attention to detail, but in return your property will be well looked after.

Social Welfare Tenants
People may be in receipt of Social Welfare for many reasons, such as disability or retirement, this is a good reason why a negative attitude towards those who rely on the State for their income is often unjustified. Over the years we have had roughly the same level of difficulties with social welfare tenants as we have had with private renters, it's just that they tend to be different problems. The predict-able difficulties of vulnerable people on low incomes are often easier to understand and deal with than the trivial-seeming problems of those more privileged.

People who have shops don't have any aversion to doing business with anybody who has money to spend. Why should landlords be any different? Most welfare tenants are in receipt of a rent allowance. This subsidy, which makes up the bulk of their rent, is usually paid directly to the landlord by the local health board. Recent cutbacks have, however, reduced the level of subsidy and made qualifying for rent allowance more difficult. It is to be hoped that these changes will soon be reversed.

AM I CUT OUT TO BE A LANDLORD?

Personal considerations play their part in the decision to buy and let property. Many investors are looking for something more interesting to do with their money than just stash it away and forget about it. Forgive me if this sounds sexist, but I think women in particular, like the idea of providing someone else with a roof over their heads. From medieval innkeepers to today's urban sophisticates looking for spacious loft-style apartments there has always been a need for people to provide accommodation to others in exchange for money, giving them a decent place to make a home.

Is becoming a landlord for you? You will need a certain amount of discipline to do well in the property business which has been aptly described as *'easy but not simple'*.

Like any other business, you will not survive if you cannot manage your cashflow. It is tempting to spend the cash as it comes in, but you must put it aside to your loan repayments, maintenance costs, professional fees and, of course, tax.

To be successful in any business you must be businesslike. Just as important in this business is that you should actually like property. Can you imagine yourself trailing through showhouses on a wet Sunday? Do you enjoy wandering through the home furnishing departments of stores and DIY shops? Do you appreciate, at a basic, gut level, the importance of a secure roof over your head? Do you find that, when it comes to property and houses, the line between work and enjoyment becomes blurred? If you could answer at least some question in the affirmative then perhaps you should consider it especially if you have other relevant skills such as a *'can do'* attitude and the ability to deal with people from a wide variety of social and cultural backgrounds.

An organised way of working is also an advantage. That said, I know at least one landlord who manages a whole portfolio of properties with the aid of only the backs of a half a dozen envelopes and a mobile phone. I wouldn't, however, recommend this business model to anybody who puts a value on peace of mind or has a memory as bad as mine.

> **Remember**
> The letting business is easy but not simple.

TAKING THE PLUNGE

Given that the arguments of investing in property are so persuasive, what's the problem? Why not go out, buy a place as cheaply as you can, spend as little as possible on it and rent it out to as many people as will fit into it? Rents, as we all know, are high these days, so you will be laughing all the way to the bank, right? In some ways it *is* that simple. It's difficult to go disastrously wrong financially when it comes to property. Unless you allow yourself to become vastly overextended, you are very unlikely to loose your shirt.

House prices crash when a large number of people become overburdened with debt on their property and the system becomes unsustainable. However, most experts are now agreed that price collapse is highly unlikely in the Irish property market, though prices are not expected to continue to rise at the same rate as recent years. It is precisely because being a landlord appears so easy, many small investors are now entering the market and investing in the large number of big apartment blocks being built in our cities and towns. As a result, tenants have a much greater choice than before, so that letting has become much more competitive. All businesses have to adjust to changing markets. All business people have to take risks. There are no guarantees in life though some investment advisors have made a great deal of money persuading people otherwise.

Chapter 8
Finding the Right Property

Nobody wants to appear stupid or slow witted. '*Location, location, location,*' they say, as if that explained everything. Funny how some phrases can be used to obscure rather than illuminate. A nodding, head and murmured agreement is often the reaction when this old chestnut is trotted out to suggest that the charms of a particular property are obvious when, in fact, they may not be at all obvious.

Finding the right property is crucial to your success as a landlord. Just as there are right and wrong ways of dealing with tenants, there are good and bad investment properties and locations. I have seen many people get it right but many more get it totally wrong. Be prepared to spend a few weeks, or months, depending on how much time you can afford, getting to know your market. Talk to estate agents and auctioneers as often as possible and read as much as you can in order to educate yourself about the letting market in general terms and about your own area in particular. Go to see places that are for sale. Don't worry too much at this stage about refining your choice, as you will gradually begin to see things more clearly when you have more information.

Case Study

Derek, father of Beth, Katie and Brian is nearing the end of his teaching career. When his children were small he began to take stock of his family's financial position and realised that if he didn't do something he wouldn't be able to educate them the way he felt he should, the way he had been educated himself. A few years later when he inherited some money he considered taking out an insurance policy to cover this future expense. On the advice of a friend, however, he decided to dip his toe in the property market instead. He bought a small, modern townhouse, topping up his inheritance with a loan from his building society and, after painting it, let it out at the going rate. Not only is he now able to finance his kids in college, but also in a position to indulge his passion for travel when his teaching job permits. More importantly, he now owns outright his own home and the second house, a valuable asset worth €300,000, for which he paid €13,000. Derek, like many others, has benefited from both rental return and capital appreciation. He bought the second property at a time when prices were low and has done very well as a result. Someone beginning now has to contend with much higher capital outlay to get started and a more competitive rental market. Don't be deterred, however, there is the advantage of low interest rates and remember, all market conditions are temporary.

A GOOD BUY?

The priorities of someone renting a house or apartment are often very different to those who seek to purchase it as their own home. Convenience and price are the factors that matter most to renters. Put yourself into the mind of a tenant in order to get a clear picture of where the market is strongest in your area.

As a novice landlord, I would suggest that you stay in your own city or town. The advantages are obvious. You know your own place, what type of people live where, how good the public transport is and what facilities are available locally – pubs, restaurants, cinemas, and so on. You are also more likely to know a reliable small builder, plumber, electrician and cleaners on your own turf and this will make managing the property much easier. In addition, you will be in a better position to know a bargain when you see one, as there is no substitute for a good local knowledge when it comes to seeking out buy-to-let property.

If you talk to estate agents who know the local market, they will advise you on the letting potential in specific places. A good agent will help clear your mind about what sort of tenants – families, singles, etc. – are most likely to want to live in different areas. Not all estate agents, however, are equally au fait with the residential letting market as it is fairly specialised. Get to know which estate agents in your town are the best for your purposes and which you can get along with most successfully. An atmosphere of trust is essential. It acts like a lubricant, eliminating a great deal of the stress associated with the business. In talking to estate agents, there are some questions you need to ask.

- What properties are on the market in my town?
- How much are these properties selling for?
- How many of them are rented?
- What rents are they achieving?
- How long does it take to rent them?
- What proportion of the year are they vacant?
- What sort of people rent them?

Agents will do their best to steer you in the right direction and it is a good idea to talk to several and evaluate what each of them says. Each will have his or her own insights to offer regarding the potential of the various properties on their books.

Remember
Beware of any property described as a 'good investment' – often there is very little else to be said for it.

Most of the newcomers to the buy-to-let market in recent times have opted for three or four-bedroomed houses or two-bedroomed custom-built apartments in mature locations. A comfortable suburb some distance from the city centre seem ideal. Traditional flats were judged too difficult to manage and new apartments too expensive to buy. The idea was to let the house to a family or young professionals who would be no trouble and would keep the place well. This proved a good strategy and can still be an excellent investment option. Even now, when many agents and landlords are worried about an oversupply, there is still a lot to recommend this segment of the market. Such properties need little management when the initial letting is set up with both sides clear on their rights and obligations. Those who seek a comfortable, secure, resting place for a lump sum could still do a lot worse. The difficult part is finding tenants for this type of property in a sluggish market. There are indications that this, the upper end of the rental market, is slow in some places. Too many landlords are chasing too few tenants. A landlord who is not burdened with large repayments either because the property was inherited or because he had a lump sum to invest, can afford to let such a property at a reasonable rent.

The chances of finding tenants quickly can, however, be greatly enhanced by attention to detail in the décor. Cast a shrewd eye on the market in your area and consider where the demand lies for this property: families, singles, students or others. Furnish and decorate the place with the most likely tenant in mind. Chapter 14 will give you some ideas on presenting your property. Magazines and the property sections of newspapers should give you some good ideas too. Then you will have a head start over the other available properties as few people bother to make the most of the rental properties they put on the market, despite the slowdown in this segment.

IDENTIFYING YOUR MARKET
Location
For those of us who don't have access to large amounts of cash or haven't inherited a property, the initial outlay for the traditional three- or four-bedroomed suburban house or custom-built apartment can be challenging. When repayments have to be made from the rent, 'letability' has to be a prime consideration. In the current rental climate, maintaining full, or almost full, occupancy rates requires a great deal of focus when letting. It is necessary to fine-tune operations, targeting particular niche markets, and become more aware that tenants want to be in areas with facilities specific to their needs.

Students, for example, will not want to live very far from the college – where the action is – no matter how good the public transport to another area. Young, working people want bars, nightclubs, cinemas and restaurants nearby, while families need schools, supermarkets and buses. There is simply no point in looking for a particular type of tenant and offering him or her the wrong sort of place.

How Much Rent?

When you have discovered what is available in your town the next thing you must do is ascertain the going rents for various areas. You may be surprised to find that more expensive properties don't necessarily give higher rent yields, not sufficiently high to warrant the additional expense at any rate. Cheaper places often fetch proportionally higher rents, especially if they have the advantage of being nearer to a town centre or large workplace.

Potential Tenants

The size of the pool of potential renters is important too. It is a fundamental principle that there are, always and everywhere, more people looking for one-bedroomed flats and small houses than larger units. While in no way wishing to endorse lower standards, it needs to be remembered that price is a major consideration for many people. The market (mainly corporate) for large, expensive properties is very limited.

The Right Property

Don't be despondent if the right property is not available immediately. It often takes months to find what you want. Personally, I would consider only about 1 per cent of the available properties at any one time as viable. In addition to your chat with your local estate agents, you should study the local papers. Check out the *'property to let'* and *'apartments and flats'* columns. Ring the telephone numbers in the advertisements to ascertain the going rents. Ask questions tailored to your target renter, such as *'Is there a large workplace in the area such as an IT company employing young graduates?'*; *'Where are the nearest schools?'*; *'How far is this property from the college?'*

Do not reject unusual places. Jenny, a young executive, was very happy living over a shop, sharing with her two friends in a busy suburban location. The shop was very convenient and the cinema nearby was an added bonus. You should also put a rogue ad in the local papers yourself to judge the response. This is a good way to ascertain the level of demand for a particular type of property or a specific location. Place the ad for a week, as some days are better then others, and you can usually get a cheaper rate for a full week's advertising. Use a phone number, nobody answers box numbers today, and you can, if you wish, leave the calls to your answering service. Six or more calls in a day indicate a very good demand in an area.

If you are an experienced landlord there is absolutely no reason not to consider a property in another city or town. If it is a good enough buy, the property can be managed successfully by an agent.

Remember
Identify the largest market in your area and go for it –
students, working singles, corporate lets or welfare recipients.

PROPERTY TYPES

There are, broadly speaking, five different categories into which most properties fall with each appealing to a different type of tenant. Some will give better returns than others on rent while others can be relied upon to give enhanced capital appreciation. They are:

- suburban houses;
- modern apartments;
- inner-city houses;
- conversions; and
- tax-incentive properties.

Suburban Houses

We have already looked at this category. Renters in this market would be either families or a few single people renting together with each having a bedroom and sharing the facilities. These properties have been all but priced out of the rental market. This is the most common type of property and as such is the one that is most often over-subscribed. Only if you are sure that what you want is a low-involvement, long-term investment and you have enough resources to pay outgoings such as mortgages, insurance and service charges while your property lies vacant, perhaps up to one third of the time, should you consider becoming involved in this area of the market. On the positive side, unless problems peculiar to an individual tenant arise this is a low-involvement option in terms of managing the property. Most renters, who opt for this segment of the market, especially if they are families, are fairly well organised and simply want to get on with their lives without undue interference. Rent will, however, be minimal relative to capital outlay so that the main advantage is capital appreciation on the property. This means that your investment has to be a fairly long-term one. The costs of buying and selling are almost prohibitive as they are calculated as a percentage of the price. If you are fortunate enough to buy early into a new housing scheme, to buy in an up and coming area or you are just lucky, you could make a lot of money in this area of the market, but capital appreciation is notoriously difficult to predict. If it were not we would all be rich.

Modern Apartments

The letting of well-appointed, modern apartments is now facing similar problems to suburban houses. In addition, they are very dependent on company letting. At the height of the Celtic Tiger, agents couldn't get enough of them, however supply has, to an extent, matched demand in this area. Their popularity was boosted by incoming executives accustomed to apartment living in the US and Europe who felt at home with the lifestyle apartments offer. They were put off by the obligation involved in the maintenance of the garden that invariably came with a house. With multinationals cutting back on employment and some executives now commuting, Monday to Friday to this country rather than uprooting themselves and their families, the apartment market is contracting. Also, apartments have hidden costs for the investor in the form of service charges to management companies. If you are thinking about investing in a modern apartment make sure you check out financial details, such as the amount of money in the contingency fund. This covers items such as roof repairs, which can land you, the landlord, with very large bills – not the tenant because in all letting agreements the fabric of the building is the landlord's responsibility. Beware too of certain locations. Many new apartments have been built in business districts so that people could live near their work. In reality, however, many of these areas are arid and impersonal, lacking even basic facilities like local shops and pubs. At night they become urban wastelands, empty and unwelcoming. Most people prefer to live in areas where there is a bit of life and will put up with the inconvenience of having to travel some distance to work.

Apartments are similar to suburban houses, being on the low side in terms of landlord involvement. Tenants, however, are generally more mobile and this means more frequent letting and longer voids. Financially the return is often less than that for suburban houses. Apartments, as well as being hard to let, can be very difficult to call in terms of capital appreciation.

Inner-City Houses

Flats and inner-city houses have always been a mainstay of the letting market. Tenants in these properties will, typically, be either single people working in town or families who may be on welfare, including a rent allowance. Unlike newly built properties, most of these flats and houses need some refurbishment, or at least extensive redecoration. Refurbishment costs and ongoing repairs are fully allowable against tax on the rent you receive. There is therefore a real incentive to keep your property in good order which makes it easier to let. Other factors, like close proximity to a range of facilities, and their compact nature, making them easier to heat and clean, ensure that these houses are attractive to renters.

The level of input required of the landlord here depends very much on how the tenancy is set up and on the condition of the building. Get the tenant and the terms right at the beginning and the arrangement should be relatively trouble free. Because inner-city houses are normally smaller and cheaper than other types of property – though rents are roughly similar – the return on this property option is better than most. One word of caution about inner-city property – and this applies equally to modern apartments – make sure that the area is a comparatively safe one, in so far as any inner-city area is safe. Be prepared, as you must with any property, to sell it if the area changes dramatically after a few years.

Conversions

Conversions are typically large, older buildings split up into flats, often one to each floor. While the terms *'flat'* and *'apartment'* are interchangeable, common usage defines an apartment as a modern, custom-built unit and a flat as a traditional unit in a converted building. Much of what has been said above about inner-city houses applies equally to conversions. Many of us have lived in such a property and remember it fondly from our youth. However, you must be prepared for a very much hands-on approach to letting here. On the plus side the rental returns on your investment are usually much higher than with other types of property. Because the property is divided into several units, the rental income can be three or four times that from a similarly priced single-unit building.

Landlords are, at the time of writing, finding these smaller units easier to let than houses or apartments because they are usually cheaper and closer to city or town centre. Single people often come to favour them, having done their time in house shares. Also, when tenants are becoming increasingly choosy, it can be much easier to decorate an older flat in which a bit of character can be emphasised than a relatively bland, featureless modern apartment.

When considering a conversion be sure to have a thorough structural survey carried out by a competent engineer or surveyor. You will, or course, have any property you are considering buying thoroughly surveyed, but in the case of conversions it is more important than ever as you have no idea of the competence or otherwise of the person who carried out the original work. Remember the famous episode in *Fawlty Towers* when O'Reilly, the builder, took out a load-bearing wall and almost caused the entire building to come crashing down? Believe it or not, I have come across exactly the same thing in a building in daily use. The extraordinary thing was that the building hadn't collapsed but had soldiered on for years with an entire first floor block wall held up by nothing more than some floorboards. Properties divided into flats are often classed as *'Pre 63'* conversions. This refers to the fact that these buildings were converted prior to the enactment of the 1963 Planning Act, which came into effect in October 1964. Buildings divided into separate units after this date require planning permission and your engineer and/or solicitor will have to be satisfied that any divisions are legal and compliant with planning regulations. You must also consider fire regulations. Some conversions are compliant with the highest standards though sadly, not all. You can, of course bring the building up to standard. This investment could, in itself, give excellent returns in capital appreciation as there is a premium on fully compliant properties.

Case Study

John and Emma had recently inherited a family home in a
rural area. They were already comfortably off and had no
immediate need for the extra cash that could be raised by
selling the property. Having no experience in the property
market they sought advice from local friends and relatives. The
advice was, overwhelmingly, to sell the property as it would be
next to impossible to find tenants in such a remote location.
Being emotionally attached to the property they were reluctant
to take this advice and advertised the property to let in a local
paper. Within a week it was let to a writer who sought an out-
of-the-way place to work on his book. When the book was
finished they had no difficulty in re-letting to a local person
returning to his roots who was in the process of buying a site
and building a house. John and Emma have been successfully
letting that house for almost 10 years now.

Despite flying in the face of two of the basic tenets of the
landlord's code – never buy a property to let in an out of the
way location and never let a property in which you have an
emotional stake, John and Emma's venture paid off mainly
because there was a dearth of property in that particular area.
They were also easygoing about how the place was kept. Not
having any neighbours to worry about was an advantage.

Often when former family homes are being let, fear of
inconvenience to neighbours is a major constraint. Landlords
who have difficulty disassociating themselves from a property
in which they have an emotional stake create a nightmare for
property managers. Every weed in the garden, every mark on
the wall, even reports of tenants returning home at night and
being a bit noisy drives the owners mad. They cannot stop
themselves worrying about the neighbours and comparing the
state of the place with how it was when their mother/father or
whoever lived in it. Don't go there. Better to sell the place and
use the money to buy another property in which you have no
personal interest. Better still, sell it and use the cash as a
deposit on two places!

Tax Incentive Property

In an effort to encourage development in certain areas, the government offered tax incentives to the purchaser of residential property for letting. See Chapter 9 for details.

CALCULATING YIELD

As we have seen, capital appreciation and rental returns or '*yield*' vary depending on type of property you choose. You can, at this point, use a formula to calculate gross yield on any property. Gross yield is defined as:

$$\frac{\text{yearly rent x 100}}{\text{price of property}} = \text{gross yield}$$

For example:

$$\frac{\text{€12,000 x 100}}{\text{€300,000}} = 4\%$$

€12,000 being the annual rent and €300,000 being the purchase price.

Looked at another way: to calculate gross yield divide the purchase price by 100 (move your decimal point back two places) and this figure is the monthly rent which will give you a gross yield of 12 per cent. Half of that will yield 6 per cent gross, and so on.

Yield can also be stated as the time it takes to recover your initial outlay on the property.

$$\frac{1}{\text{gross yield}} = \text{payback time}$$

In our example above the payback period is 25 years.

Gross yield is not the same as *net* yield. To calculate net yield expenses must be deducted from the gross yield. Add together the following costs:

• professional fees (other than those connected with the initial purchase and setting up of the property);

- management charges (on apartments);
- any electricity and gas for which the landlord is liable;
- refuse collection (where applicable);
- ground rent (where applicable);
- maintenance, wear and tear and redecoration;
- insurance;
- cleaning;
- advertising; and
- agency fees (if using a letting agent).

Do not include mortgage repayments. Deduct the total from the gross rent and proceed as above – dividing the balance by the current value of the house and multiplying by 100 to get a percentage. Very roughly speaking, net yield should be about two thirds of gross yield.

Taxation matters will be looked at again in Chapter 11, but at this juncture, before you take fright and abandon the whole idea, you need to know that the picture is not as bleak as it might appear. Almost all of the ongoing costs outlined above and also interest on borrowings associated with the property are fully allowable against the income tax due on rental income. In the case of capital items such as furniture, depreciation is allowed over a period of eight years. In addition a loss made in one year can be carried forward to subsequent years.

Unless you have very deep pockets try to go for a *'cash positive'* investment. This means an investment where the rent will, at least, cover all of your outgoings including your mortgage payments. While *'gross yield'* and *'net yield'* are technical concepts, the bottom line for you, the property owner, is whether you can at least remain solvent and be able to sleep peacefully in your bed at night.

Exceptions to the *'cash positive'* rule might be considered in some circumstances, either (a) where projected capital appreciation is strong enough to justify subsidising the project from personal funds or (b) where the objective is a low-involvement, long-term investment.

Remember
Go for a cash positive investment if at all possible.

VIEWING A PROPERTY

When considering a property do not be afraid to ask to see it several times. Make a checklist of the accommodation, taking the following into account.

The Kitchen

Is it bright? It is difficult to make dark kitchens look clean. Is it big enough for a small table and chairs? Are the units OK or do they need replacing? Will replacing the doors be enough? Is there enough space for the basics – a fridge, cooker and storage area?

Bathroom

Do the fittings need replacing? Is the floor sound? Wooden floors often rot in bathrooms. Is there a shower? A power shower is very desirable these days. Is there sufficient light and ventilation? Ventilation can be installed in the shape of an extractor fan, specially designed for the purpose, if there is no window.

Bedrooms

Make sure the smallest bedroom is big enough for a bed and some sort of wardrobe. Do not be afraid to change the use of rooms. An inadequate bedroom can be used as something else, perhaps a study, and a sitting room can be converted into a bedroom if the kitchen is big enough to become a kitchen/living room.

Heating

Is there an adequate heating system or is it old and in need of replacement? In flats electric storage heating is usually the safest and best option. In larger, single unit buildings natural gas is probably cheaper to run.

Electrics

Is the fuse board of the old type, the one with porcelain cylinders? Modern fuse boards have switches. Old wiring and fuse boards will need to be replaced. Don't forget that the ESB has stringent regulations regarding fire safety in relation to its own installations. If they are not happy they won't connect you until you bring the place up to their exacting standards. Talk to your surveyor or electrician about this.

Is it a Listed Building?

Before you dismiss the idea as being of relevance only to buildings of great historic significance be aware that many quite ordinary buildings are now listed. Have your surveyor check this out, as the owners of such buildings are greatly limited in the use of their property. Refurbishment and even minor repairs often need planning permission and can be very costly.

Finding the right property is not easy. It usually takes time. It is often a good idea to go for rental income rather than capital appreciation. So far in modern times in this country all properties have risen in value. If the capital appreciation turns out to be above average for that type of property or area, regard that as a bonus, not something that you can really plan for. Many people have bought into areas they believed to be up-and-coming, only to find they would need to live to be about 150 for the area to finally make it to the finish line. My personal view, which is of course only one opinion, is that my business is letting property so I concentrate on rent. When I hear people say they wouldn't let a place they wouldn't live in themselves I wonder, 'Why not?' If I ran a fashion shop I wouldn't expect to be able to wear everything in stock. I will let anything that someone else will live in, so long as it's up to a basic standard of safety, comfort and cleanliness.

Remember
Determine your main goal:
- regular monthly income;
- long-term capital appreciation; or
- tax shelter.

Chapter 9
Financing Your Investment

PROPERTY PRICE RISES
The Big Picture
Successful property investment, whether for your own use or for rental purposes, requires at least a passing knowledge of how prices fluctuate over time. Armed with a broader, longer term view of the market we can avoid becoming agitated by every breeze that comes our way, make wiser choices and minimise stress and worry in the process.

According to the *The Economist* (29 August 2002) people in the developed world own US$23 trillion in equities, but US$40 trillion in property, making property the world's biggest asset class. With the exception of Japan and Germany, house prices have consistently outpaced inflation since the Second World War. A study recently undertaken by the Milken Institute in Los Angeles suggests that, in the US, housing has replaced gold as a safe repository of wealth in times of uncertainty. This is justified by the fact that Americans have seen prices rise more between 1997 and 2002 than in any previous five-year period since 1945. A survey of Irish house prices published in *The Sunday Times* (2 November 2003) concluded that Irish property is among the most expensive in Europe. Dublin, it seems, beats Berlin and Paris hands down even though average incomes here are lower. House price inflation rose from 2 per cent in 1993 to 15 per cent in 1996 to a whopping 30 per cent in 1998. In 2003 the housing price index (according to Permanent TSB/ESRI figures) stood at approximately 14 per cent. Dr Brendan Walsh, Professor of Economics at University College Dublin, believes that house prices here are expensive compared to many other countries, but maybe, he suggests, like the south of England or most big cities, Ireland is just a very desirable place to live. Other less-sanguine experts are talking about a property bubble and forecasting a crash. Most believe, however, that the current surge is nothing more than part of the usual cyclical nature of price rises, albeit more exaggerated than normal – a dramatic rise followed by a slow down, followed in turn by a period of stagnation before the cycle begins again.

The property market is characterised by continuous change. In the late eighties and early nineties, it was extremely difficult to sell any property other than something small and cheap. That now feels like the remote and distant past. As an auctioneer I tried very hard at that time to get decent prices for some lovely properties. A beautiful three-storey Victorian house, less than five minutes from University College Cork and 10 minutes from the city centre, proved impossible to sell at £65,000, while £50,000 was too much for an elegant, detached house with a fine garden in Douglas, a prestigious suburb of Cork. When you've been around the market for a few years you realise that, in some ways, the more things change, the more they stay the same. While fundamental shifts do, without doubt, take place – we may have witnessed one such in relation to lower interest rates – it is generally as a result of major political or social change. When we joined the Eurozone we nailed our colours to the same mast as France and Germany, and we now enjoy low interest as a result. Estate agents have a vested interest in being upbeat about the market and newspapers have to be ever vigilant about their circulation figures. It is essential for them to be at all times interesting and, whenever possible, sensational. Picture the headline *'House Prices Normal!'* How exciting is that? Beware of journalistic hype.

A Closer Look
A few facts, which affect the housing market in Ireland, are beyond doubt.

• We still have a young population relative to other countries in Europe. Economically and socially a young population is the biggest boon any country could have. Not only is there someone to look after us in our old age and we have the joy of young blood in our midst, but we are also guaranteed a continuing demand for all sorts of goods and services. This is what keeps any economy vibrant. What could be better for the housing market than a steady stream of young people setting up home and raising families?

• Interest rates are currently at their lowest level in 40 years. While house prices are at an all-time high, a new factor, *affordability*, has entered the equation. Current low rates, combined with rising salaries and relatively low income tax have put property within reach of a whole new generation which, a decade ago, would have emigrated.

• Our economy is the envy of our European partners. While this remains the case we can probably look forward to an increase in immigration in years to come. Up to now we have had a small number of immigrants by European standards. They have come mainly from Africa, the Far East and Eastern Europe, many of them arriving here as asylum seekers. Despite recent legal changes to discourage an influx, with the expansion of the European Community we can expect a number of Eastern Europeans to migrate here to live and work.

• While the level of borrowings has risen, the all important loan-to-value ratio currently stands at a healthy 65 per cent. Commentators, considering the rise in levels of mortgage lending here in the past 12 months, have been reminding us of the crash in British house prices in the late eighties. The problem then was negative equity, where people had houses which were worth less than the amount they had borrowed on them. This is unlikely here as overall the loan-to-value ratio is quite high. It would take a major crash, where prices would drop more than 30 per cent overall for negative equity to be a problem in this country.

These facts augur very well for the continuing health of the Irish market and suggest a price crash is unlikely in the foreseeable future.

RENTAL RETURNS
When I first became interested in renting property I was considering purchasing properties whose prices were pitched at seven times the

annual rent. In real terms, paying a mortgage, maintenance costs and tax on the rental income meant that a well-run property would pay for itself in about 10 or 11 years. In the early nineties, a small terraced house could be bought for about £25,000 and rented for about £380 a month, yielding a whopping 18.24 per cent. Since then property prices have soared and rents have not kept pace, despite what we read and hear about landlords ripping off vulnerable tenants. Peter Bacon, the economist who was commissioned by the government to study the Irish housing market in the late nineties, found that rents in this country were low by comparison with the rest of Europe. When we consider the rate of price increases outlined above we realise that capital appreciation, even if only at an average level, is the real story today, the driving force that makes becoming a landlord a worthwhile proposition.

THE MORTGAGE MAZE

If you have huge amounts of money in your bank account do not bother to read this section. Most of us, however, live less privileged lives. We need the assistance of financial institutions and to take risks in order to fund our property acquisitions. In Chapter 2 we discussed the basics of applying for a mortgage and calculating how much you could expect to be offered by a lender. Anyone considering a buy-to-let mortgage will, I presume, have already secured his own home.

Contrary to popular belief, and unlike other types of investment and most businesses, property has the advantage of being an easy investment area to get into. This idea might come as a shock to people struggling to buy their first home and I don't wish to appear insensitive (having been there, I do appreciate how stressful it is) but people differ widely in their attitude to stress. A 50-year-old who has been through the process of buying and selling property a few times will have quite a different perspective to someone starting out.

Mortgages have a negative image. Being generally associated with the curtailment of freedom as young people begin to settle down and take on adult responsibilities, they have as much charm as an albatross. With a little knowledge and self-confidence, however, we can use financial institutions to our advantage. A basic understanding of mortgages and the *'nuts and bolts'* of finance is essential in order to be able to put the system to work for you. Later I will suggest ways for you to proceed even if you don't have money for a deposit on a property, but let's assume for now that you have the required minimum of 10 per cent of the market price of the property of your choice.

Annuity and Interest-Only Mortgages

Both of these mortgage types are very popular with buy-to-let investors. The annuity mortgage is the traditional mortgage, ideally suited to you if you are buying your own home or a single property to let. The monthly payment includes both interest and capital. At the end of the term of the mortgage you will own the property outright. With the interest-only type interest is paid monthly but no payments are made towards the capital. This mortgage is designed with investors in mind because monthly repayments are low which means they can usually be covered by the rent.

The interest-only mortgage is particularly suited to you if you are investing in a number of properties where capital appreciation is your main incentive as when you sell the property you benefit from the increase in price, repaying only the amount borrowed. Usually it is possible to convert to a standard annuity mortgage at any time during the life of an interest-only mortgage. This is often a good idea as rent increases make it easier to make repayments as time goes on. Alternatively, an interest-only mortgage may be kept going almost indefinitely while inflation erodes the value of the amount borrowed. This type of loan may, in certain limited circumstances, be suited to the owner-occupier as it keeps monthly payments to a minimum. The disadvantage, however, is that since no capital repayments are made, the original loan remains unpaid. An investor is in a different position, however, as the interest on the loan is fully allowable against tax due on rent.

Endowment Mortgage

With this mortgage the monthly payment is actually a premium paid into an insurance policy which should, in theory, mature to the value of the capital borrowed and the interest which accrued. These were popular in the seventies and eighties but have fallen out of favour in recent years as most of the policies failed on maturity to match the amount outstanding, leaving the householders to come up with the additional lump sum at the point where they expected to be free of mortgage repayments.

Current Account Mortgage

Finally, a new type of mortgage has recently arrived on the scene, the so-called '*current account mortgage*'. The unique feature of this product is that both the current account and mortgage account are linked together. This enables the customer to borrow from the equity in the property simply by writing a cheque. Up to 75 per cent of the current market value of the property can be borrowed with very few formalities. The advantages are obvious at a time when property prices are rising. Money can be borrowed at mortgage rates, about half of what is usual for personal loans. The disadvantage is that considerable discipline is needed when cash is so readily available. It represents a real boon for those who can put their money to good use, a disaster for those who fear that money burns a hole in their pocket.

How Much Can You Borrow?

Today it is not uncommon to borrow 90 per cent or even 92 per cent of the purchase price of a property plus costs. The amount you can borrow is based on a multiple of your income – usually 2.5–3 times the basic salary plus once a second salary. Most lenders will insist that you be in permanent full-time employment in order to qualify. For the self-employed the figure is usually based on an average of your last three years' accounts.

Mortgages and Self-Direct Trusts

With a pension mortgage the term of the loan is fixed to coincide with the holder's expected retirement date. It contains elements of the interest-only and the endowment mortgage in that the borrower pays only the interest due on the loan and also a premium into a personal pension plan. This premium qualifies for tax relief, making it a very tax-efficient type of mortgage for some. At the end of the term the holder receives a 25 per cent tax-free lump sum from the accumulated fund. Though not guaranteed, and certain advisers are eager to point this out, it is expected that the lump sum will be enough to cover the mortgage.

Pension mortgages do not suit everyone. As with endowment mortgages there is a risk that the fund will not grow sufficiently to cover the loan in full. Also a relatively large monthly payment must be made to cover both the loan interest and the premium. This is why these pensions are offered mainly to high-net worth individuals such as company directors, business proprietors and senior employees.

In the 2004 Finance Act changes were made to the rules for self-administered pensions. Money may now be borrowed, with the fund as security, and used to purchase property.

When the pension fund has grown enough to cover the deposit on a property, the remainder of the purchase price may be borrowed under the terms of the self-administered pension scheme and the tax relief availed of.

Professional financial advice is essential for this type of structured investment.

Interest Rates

Interest rate levels in Ireland are now dictated by the European Central Bank which is, in turn, influenced by the international economy which causes rates to rise and fall in a cyclical manner. The length of these cycles is notoriously difficult to predict. In the late eighties interest rates briefly reached 15 per cent. Now, at about 4 per cent they are at their lowest level for over 40 years.

Make sure you get the best rate going at the time. You can do this by checking the figures listed in the papers. Mortgages can be *'fixed'*, *'variable'* or linked to the ECB base rate, called the *'tracker'* rate. When interest rates are low it is best to choose a fixed rate, typically, for one, three or five years, after which it reverts to the variable rate. Many people like the security of a fixed rate as it makes it easier to budget when they know exactly how much the mortgage will cost each month.

Using a Mortgage Broker

A good broker, one who specialises in mortgages, can save you a great deal of time and frustration. I would urge everyone to get the best possible advice at all stages of purchasing property. You need a broker who has access to a variety of lenders' products, rather than one who is tied to one lender. Some charge a small arrangement fee, though most do not.

Getting the borrowing right is essential. This does not, of course, mean borrowing as much as possible all of the time. Personal levels of comfort come into the picture too. One person will have no difficulty with borrowings of a million or two, while others with more modest loans will be petrified with worry and anxiety.

TAX-EFFICIENT PROPERTY INVESTMENTS
Section 23

In an effort to improve the stock of rental properties, the government introduced a number of measures which provided special tax relief on property investments. Section 23, as the original and best of these schemes is called, introduced in the early eighties, has led to a major improvement in the quality of rented accommodation in this country and has changed the face of many of our cities and towns for the better.

Other schemes cover specific areas of the property market. These, with their cut-off dates, are listed in Appendix 2. At the time of writing, most are due to end on 31 December 2004 but they have already been extended a number of times and are currently under review. They are of interest here because qualifying properties may be bought and sold after that date, any unused tax relief being transferred to the new owner. The advantage of these schemes is that capital outlay, less the cost of the site, may be claimed as an allowance against the income tax due on rent. The main condition attaching to the schemes is that the property must be let in full for 10 years from the date of completion.

An important point for holders of a number of rented properties to note is that the relief can be spread over all rental profits from any source in the Republic of Ireland. A property with unused tax relief could be a good buy if the price is right. Often, however, the tax savings are factored into the price of such properties and as a result they are not as desirable as they may at first appear. It is essential to get advice from a tax consultant on these matters as the rules governing tax-relief schemes are quite technical.

Refurbished Residential Rental Property

Tax relief is available for the refurbishment of any rented residential property in Ireland. Expenditure on any reconstruction, repair and renewal is allowed against the tax due on all rental income. These capital allowances are spread over seven years. The refurbishment must be in accordance with the guidelines for rented property issued by the Department of the Environment, Housing & Local Government. As with Section 23, the property must be let for 10 years, though again, it may be sold, with the relief passing to the new owner.

Section 50: Student Accommodation

This scheme applies only to new, purpose-built accommodation within a radius of 8 kilometres from a third-level college. There must be a minimum of 20 bed spaces in all. Again, as with Section 23, Section 50 allows for qualifying expenditure to be offset against all rental income. Other rules and specifications apply and are available from the Department of the Environment, Housing & Local Government. It is important to note that full planning must have been received before 31 May 2003 for a Section 50 scheme to be valid.

Other Tax-Efficient Investments

Other reliefs similar to sections 23 and 50 are available though with differing rules and regulations which must be satisfied. They include relief for investment in nursing homes and housing units for the elderly, multi-storey car parks, childcare facilities and sports-injury clinics. Contact your tax adviser to discuss what is suitable for you.

A full list of all Special Tax Reliefs currently available for property Investment along with their cut off dates appears in Appendix 2.

Caution

When assessing tax-driven property investment consider carefully the price being asked for the property. As any financial adviser will tell you, an investment must make sense in its own terms regardless of the tax breaks. Tax relief is a bonus. Consider the yield and potential for capital growth from the property in its own right and don't get carried away with the tax issue. Some investors, and indeed some advisers, become obsessed with saving tax almost to the exclusion of all other considerations. Builders and developers are very much aware of this phenomenon and they will often push property solely on the basis of the tax breaks. As a result, many section properties are overpriced for the areas in which they are built. A friend who considered investing in one commented, '*It's a bit like spending a euro to save 50 cents.*' Make sure that you are the one who stands to benefit most from the tax-incentives, not the developer.

Case Study

When their two children were small, John and Elaine wanted
to ensure they had something put aside for when they grew
up. Working hard at their careers, his in the bank and hers as
a GP, they liked having enough cash for what they wanted like
family holidays and hobbies. John enjoyed collecting things,
telescopes, ancient Roman artefacts and old technology. Her
idea of relaxation was to dabble in painting and pottery. Their
tax bills were high and growing as their salaries increased.
Last year they decided to invest in property. There were
several new housing schemes, close to where they lived, on
the market at the time and they felt somewhere near home
would be easier to manage. Being realistic people they had
reservations. They knew that letting could be a problem a bit
out from the city and given the high-profile nature of their
jobs they worried that dealing with tenants might be difficult.
They decided to take advice from a friend who was a director
of one of the larger estate agencies around. 'Buy a tax-
efficient apartment,' he suggested, 'A Section 50 will give good
capital appreciation and will cut out tax on the rent.'

An ideal apartment scheme had just begun. Attached to
the local university, not only was there a ready-made
student market, but under a management deal their friend's
company would guarantee a certain level of rent and offer a
full management service. As things now stand, they have
paid €200,000 for a one-bedroomed apartment. When site
costs of €24,000 for which there is no tax allowance is
excluded, the figure of €176,000 can be offset over 10 years
against their rental income. This is in addition to the usual
items that can be set off such as the costs of management
and repairs. This represents a good investment, assuming
there is a rental market for the apartment. They have been
careful not to overextend themselves and can comfortably
cover a few months' repayments should the apartment
remain vacant.

GETTING STARTED

Don't be too limited in your thinking when it comes to finding the initial investment capital required to purchase your property. There are always things you can do with money to put it to more efficient use. If finding a deposit is a problem you might consider some of the following strategies.

Strategy 1: Remortgage Your Existing Property

If you already own a property, your own home for example, the whole property can be remortgaged and the equity tied up in your home released. An alternative is to raise a second loan on the property, keeping your existing mortgage and borrowing on the remaining equity in the property. This is a particularly useful means of raising cash at a time of rapidly rising house prices. The risks are minimal as the second property can always be sold if things don't work out as planned. Any losses incurred should be more than covered by the rise in property prices in the meantime.

Where you will come unstuck with this strategy is in the unlikely event of a price collapse. However, unless you have sailed very close to the wind indeed, borrowing up to the limit, which is never a good idea, loans can be renegotiated until there is an upturn. If you leave a little slack and are in a position to cover three to six months' repayments without any rent coming in then you should be fine.

Strategy 2: Get a 100 Per Cent Mortgage

You can, especially from financial institutions that are newcomers to the Irish market, get a 100 per cent mortgage. However, there is usually a stipulation that you will live in the property yourself, but there is, or course, nothing to prevent you from occupying one bedroom and letting out the other rooms. In time, when the mortgage company is satisfied that you are making your repayments as agreed and you have built up a good reputation, there shouldn't be any problem if you tell them you have decided to let the entire property. The institution may want to charge you an increased rate of interest, but you can argue your case. Don't accept everything they tell you as gospel. Like everybody else in business they have to be flexible. Remember too that all money paid out as interest is fully deductible against tax on rents.

Strategy 3: Revaluing Your Property

A third strategy involves revaluing your property and can be used in conjunction with strategies one and two to expand your portfolio of properties. You bought your first property for, say €200,000. In two years it will have increased in value by, say €42,000 at a very modest rate of 10 per cent a year. By applying to your mortgage company for a revaluation you should be able to continue with your current level of repayment and have the €42,000 released as a deposit for another property. This is the essence of *'gearing'* in property terms. The danger with this strategy is that you might, having got the knack, overextend yourself. Be sure to have enough slack to cover about six months' repayments.

Other Strategies

For further tips on securing initial funding see *'Finding the Deposit'* in Chapter 3.

Case Study

Consider the hypothetical stories of Jerry and Marianne.

Jerry

Jerry, who had been living in a rented flat, inherited €150,000 and decided to buy an apartment. When he approached his bank manager to discuss how much he could draw down as a mortgage he was surprised that he was only offered €65,000 and he wondered how he could have managed without the inheritance. Jerry's salary as a teacher was, at the time, €25,000 annually. His bank manager was willing to advance a little over 2.5 times his salary. With a total of €212,500 to spend he decided on a modest apartment near Limerick City for €195,000 which left him with slightly less than enough to cover his costs – stamp duty, solicitor's and surveyor's fees and so on. To furnish the apartment and make it reasonably comfortable, he had to resort to the time-honoured practice of first-time buyers, doing up a room at a time and cadging discarded furniture and equipment from relatives. Unfortunately this meant that he was unable to rent out a room to help with the mortgage.

His financial position, as a result of these transactions looks something like this:

Monthly Repayments (allowing for tax rebate): €270.000
Income from property: Nil

Marianne

Marianne inherited the same amount, namely €150,000. Instead of buying one house she opted for three different properties. The first was an ex-corporation house close to the city centre for which she paid €190,000. Second she purchased a pre-'63 conversion, laid out in four units for €300,000 and finally she bought a modern apartment for €200,000, a total of €690,000 for all three. All of her purchases were funded by mortgages from different financial institutions. Using €69,000 of her inheritance as a 10 per cent deposit and borrowing the remaining €621,000 left her with €81,000, the balance of her inheritance, in cash.

When all three deals were completed Marianne's financial position now looked something like this:

Monthly Mortgage Payments: €2,691
Income from property: €2,816

In this scenario, Marianne lives in the apartment, her choice of property, and her mortgage repayments are more than covered by her rental income. While this income incurs a tax liability of 42 per cent the interest paid on her mortgages is fully deductible. Since, in the early stages of an annuity mortgage, almost all of the repayment is made up of interest, and is consequently allowable against tax, (see Chapter 11) this give her a net monthly balance of €125.00. In addition she has her €81,000, the balance of her inheritance in cash. With this money she can do the small amount of decoration necessary on the property and keep the rest as a hedge against periods when the properties are unlet or to cover any other contingency.

Chapter 10

Up and Running: Letting Your Property

L et us assume, for now, that your property is in good order and ready for occupation. If you are unsure on this score, check the minimum standards set by law for rented property in Chapter 11. Bear in mind that these standards are pretty basic, the absolute rock bottom that you will get away with this side of the law and just barely compatible with civilised living.

In today's competitive market it is essential to maintain a reasonable standard of décor and comfort. This need not cost the earth. *'More dash than cash'* would be a good motto. We will have a much closer look at how to present your property for letting or sale in Chapter 14. *'Staging your property'* as the practice is called in the US has almost become an art form over there.

FURNISHING
Your first consideration will be whether or not to furnish your property. There is a perception that renting an unfurnished property bestows some additional security of tenure on the renter. This is not so. Legally, whether or not a place is furnished makes no difference to the tenant's rights. Both furnished and unfurnished places are governed by the same laws and regulations. Most properties on the market are let furnished, though there is a sizeable demand for unfurnished places. Agents will tell you that the market for furnished properties is larger as many renters are transitory nowadays and don't

want to cart tons of furniture around with them. There is very little difference in rent, if any, between furnished and unfurnished places. If you are a first-time landlord your main concern will be ease and speed of letting. Though furnished properties are likely to let more quickly, the downside is the hassle of buying, maintaining and replacing things like sofas, beds, hoovers and kettles, especially if you have a number of properties.

Fiona Fullerton, journalist and property guru, always furnishes her properties as they look much better that way. Certainly, unfurnished places can look cold and forbidding when you are showing prospective tenants around. Many people are sadly lacking in the visualisation department and seem unable to recognise potential in a property. They also find it difficult to envisage their own furniture in situ. It is impossible for them to see how, for example, a three-piece suite, a sideboard and a coffee table, not to mention accessories like rugs and lamps, will fit into the living room, as spaces tend to look smaller without furniture.

Ultimately, the decision of whether or not to furnish will depend a lot on your personal inclination. Some landlords actually like the process of decorating and furnishing a property, bringing out its hidden potential and showing it to best advantage. Others haven't the remotest interest in interiors and would probably make a hames of it anyway. A place which is badly furnished, where no care has been taken to get the colours or the scale right will probably look worse than an empty one and might take longer to let as a result.

What to Include When Furnishing
Of all the issues which cause disputes between landlords and tenants, the most difficult to resolve often relates to the contents and condition of the house when the tenant is ready to move out. A detailed inventory with the condition of the items noted will make these problems less likely to occur, or at least minimise disputes when they do arise. Landlords should be aware that *'wear and tear'* is to be expected. It is, after all, part of what the tenant is paying for. The difference between normal wear and tear and damage, whether accidental or malicious, is a grey area. In general, breakages should be replaced by the tenant with similar items of equal value.

New landlords are often unsure what to include when furnishing a property. Try to get a balance between too little, which looks sparse, or too much which looks cluttered. I would suggest that you let the appearance be your guide. We live in a time when image is all-important. There seems to be no clear definition of the term *'furnished'* available and obviously there will be huge variations in the standard of fit-out depending on the type of property and the amount of the rent being asked for. The following sample inventory is intended as a rough guide only and should be seen as a fairly basic.

SAMPLE INVENTORY
Living Room
1 green-patterned sofa, good
2 plain green armchairs, good
l large green and gold rug, as new
1 side table, new
1 white wooden lamp, new
1 low bookshelf, as new
1 corner cabinet, 10 years old
1 over mantle mirror, new
1 electric fire inset, as new
1 green wastebasket
1 fire screen with pewter finish, new
1 glass light fitting, new
Carpet, curtains and drapes, good

Kitchen
1 dining table, five years old
3 kitchen chairs, five years old
1 cooker as new, all parts supplied
1 fridge, as new
1 washing machine, as new
Assorted tableware (delph)
Set of three saucepans
1 large saucepan
1 frying pan
1 baking dish
1 roasting tray
1 kettle, as new
1 microwave, new

1 mop and bucket
1 sweeping brush
1 dustpan and brush
1 vacuum cleaner, working
2 light shades
Kitchen units in good condition throughout, no handles missing

Bedroom 1
1 double bed, good
2 bedside tables, fair
2 reading lamps, new
1 wardrobe, 10 years old
1 chest, fair
2 light shades
Carpet, curtains and drapes, good

Bedroom 2
1 single bed, as new
1 desk, fair
1 corner shelf
1 locker, good
1 wardrobe, fair
1 light shade
Carpet, curtains and drapes, good

Bathroom
1 power shower, as new
1 shower curtain, white
1 waste bin
1 toilet brush in holder
2 clothes rails
1 laundry basket
Floor, one stain on tiles, none missing or cracked
All taps working
Shower, washbasin and toilet, clean and in perfect working order

Hallway
1 rug
1 light shade
1 hall table

Flooring, good except for one small tear at kitchen entrance

Signed   _____

Landlord   _____

Tenant   _____

Date   _____

USING A LETTING AGENT

Any landlord who has had to deal with a 3 a.m. call about loud music and mayhem emanating from the flat next door or a query such as, *'My cooker won't work. What will I do?'*, or the perennial, *'I can't get in, I've lost my keys'* after the pubs close, will know the value of a good management service. Having decided whether or not to furnish your property, your next consideration will be whether you want to manage your property yourself or leave it to an agent. Opinion is very much divided on this issue, but your choice will depend on the level of involvement you are comfortable with, how much time you have at your disposal and how big your business is (i.e. the number of properties or units you are letting). Those new to letting might be glad of a way of putting some distance between themselves and the tenant. The type of property and the tenant are also considerations. Some tenants resent too much contact with their landlord, seeing it as interference.

Once the tenancy is properly set up, most properties should almost manage themselves with very little effort on your part. On the other hand, a good agent can earn his fees many times over by finding a better tenant and negotiating a higher rent. Finding an agent who specialises in management can be difficult, however. Many excellent estate agents have less interest in management than in sales and straightforward letting where the day-to-day work is left to you. They often give the impression that this aspect of their business is less important than their main one and that it is more hassle than it is worth. Be careful to choose the right agent. Every effort should be made to find someone who is experienced in management. A bad tenant, left to his own devices, can cost you a great deal of money between repairs, lost rent and possible legal fees. A good compromise might be to employ someone for the letting only, doing the ongoing management yourself. Agents are at their best when negotiating deals and can be invaluable when it comes to working out the details of the letting agreement. Often they don't have the time or the patience it takes to keep your tenants happy.

Though I manage my own properties myself, using an agent has one further advantage. As with repairs, management fees are allowable against the income tax payable on the rent received. If you go it alone, on the other hand, you cannot claim a tax allowance against the value of your own work. This only matters, of course, if tax is due. If you are making large mortgage repayments then you may not, in fact, be making any profit.

Read more about tax in Chapter 11.

How to Choose an Agent

- Choose a company that specialises in property management. They will have the experience to do a good job for you and will have enough properties on their books to make it worth their while to have a dedicated staff and efficient procedures in place.
- Make sure that whoever you are considering is fully licensed and bonded. This is your only security against a conman making off with your cash. It is always best to use either a well-established firm or one which comes recommended by someone you know.
- Have a look at your local paper to see who is doing the most advertising of rental properties. An agent with full books should let a place more quickly than one with a few properties as they will be better known and will probably market the property more efficiently.
- Choose an agent with a good High Street presence if you can. Many properties are let through their appearance in the shop window.
- To ensure you are comparing like with like, find out exactly what is being offered, for example, how often the property will be inspected when it is tenanted. Are contracts arranged as part of the basic fee or do you need to consult your solicitor? This will incur extra costs, but most agents include handling the contracts as part of the letting process. Are there any additional charges? Does their quoted price include VAT? Ask for an

itemised quotation, in writing, so that you will then know precisely what is included. You can expect that the cost of all advertising and marketing of your property would be included in the basic fee.

- Most agents offer a range of services from letting only, letting and rent collection to full management. Fees vary enormously. Expect to pay from 5 per cent of the annual rent, for letting only, to 15 per cent for full management. It is tempting to choose the agent who seems to be charging least, but the chances are that the level of service is reflected in the price. Today services are expensive to provide and, as in most things, you generally get what you pay for.

- Don't give the property to more than one agent at a time. There is nothing more likely to annoy letting agents who arrive to show a property to a prospective tenant than to find another agent already there, showing it to someone else. In this situation, either the agent will feel under pressure to let the place as quickly as possible, perhaps to a less than ideal tenant or he will, if he has several properties to let, put yours on the backburner. Give him a reasonable amount of time to do what you ask of him, say a month to six weeks. Then change to another agent if you are not satisfied that your property is being given the attention it deserves.

- You need to satisfy yourself completely on two issues: that all possible precautions are taken and all checks are made to ensure a reliable tenant and second that all of your legal obligations in respect of the contract are fulfilled.

Remember
The letting agreement is between *you*, not your agent, and the tenant. It is *your* legal responsibility, nobody else's to ensure that its terms are fulfilled.

LETTING IT YOURSELF
Marketing

For most private landlords, at least those in major cities, the most effective place to advertise is in the local evening paper. The fee is generally around half that charged by the nationals and these papers have a higher local profile. When people begin to look for a house or flat this is usually the first place they look. There are, however, many other opportunities for marketing such as staff newsletters and notice boards in large, nearby workplaces. You could also try local health clubs, hospitals, schools and colleges, anywhere in fact where there is a notice board to which you can gain access. Use a clearly printed sign with tear-off strips at the bottom with your phone number printed on them. There are many other options, but most of them take more time and organisation than you probably can spare, so these measures are only worth considering when the local paper has failed to deliver a tenant. Even then, I would prefer to consider the reasons why a place is not letting.

A new shop window available in recent times, which shows promise, is the internet. E-letting has become popular with the young, computer-literate generation. For a moderate fee, or in some cases for nothing, landlords can key in what they have to offer and the expected rent. Tenants, in turn, key in their requirements and with a little luck, the result could be a marriage made in Heaven, or at least in Cyberland. Photos can be included and details updated weekly or even daily. Websites can be accessed from anywhere, worldwide, 24/7, making things much easier for people relocating from one area or country to another.

If, after a few weeks of advertising, a place is still unlet despite several enquiries and some viewings, there is something wrong. Perhaps, for some reason the area has become less desirable over time, or maybe the property needs upgrading. When someone looks at a place and decides not to take it, I always ask them why. This is market research at its best; the sort that is invaluable to me and costs large companies millions to buy.

Finding the Right Tenant Yourself

Even if you have, at this point, decided to hand your property over lock, stock and barrel to an agent, it is a good idea to read through the next section as you need to know just what your agent will be doing on your behalf. At the end of the day, this is *your* business. Even if you hand the day-to-day running over to someone else, it is in your own interest to be in a position to evaluate what is happening.

First, your mindset may need adjusting. Consider two identical properties. These are hypothetical cases, but fairly typical.

Property A

Rent:	€750 monthly
Advertising:	€20 (local paper)
Void:	none
Annual income less marketing costs:	€8,980

Property B

Rent:	€800 monthly
Advertising:	€200
Void:	1 month
Annual income less marketing costs:	€8,600

As you can see from this example, chasing the highest possible rent does not always pay. Not only will it quite often not save you money, but think of the time you save showing the property if you let it more quickly. You also end up with tenants who are happy to be getting a good deal. The last thing any landlord needs in his property is a disgruntled tenant. You are almost guaranteed to have twice as many problems with a renter who feels unfairly treated or overcharged. If he is surrounded by other tenants, as in a flat or house share, that discontent will spread like a miasma, poisoning the atmosphere and making for even more difficulties. Often too, less desirable tenants are prepared to pay higher rent as they find it difficult to get a landlord prepared to take them, but you could end up with bigger headaches and larger repair bills in the end. Asking for less rent is not, on the other hand, a sure fire way to end up with good tenants, but think of a time when you were charged less than you expected for something, or an instance when you were given money back, though it was not strictly necessary and remember the good feeling the experience engendered. Keep your tenants sweet if at all possible.

References

At least two written references, one personal, from a landlord perhaps, and a professional one from an employer are usually required from the prospective tenant. A third, from the bank would be ideal. It is, unfortunately, easy for a clever person intent on a sting to produce references. *'It's very hard to be sure about references, even when you get a phone number and check. There is no way of being sure who is at the other end of the line.'* So says a friend of mine who happens to be a letting agent.

Many landlords are paranoid about the possibility of rent not being paid. There is, of course, absolutely no way of being sure that this will never happen, whether or not you use an agent. A determined conman who sets out to do so will always be able to find a way to catch you, but sometimes we just have to be philosophical. Growing up in a shop, I remember that it was accepted that a certain percentage of the stock would be pilfered. It was good training for being a landlord. If all reasonable precautions have been taken and, in spite of it, you still become a victim, accept it as a business loss and move on.

Discrimination

When choosing a tenant, a landlord has to be careful not to discriminate against certain groups protected by law. According to equality legislation, in existence for some years now, there are nine grounds on which you are not entitled to discriminate against people, these are:

- sex;
- race;
- religion;
- marital status;
- family status;
- disability;
- age;
- sexual orientation; and
- membership of the Travelling Community.

Never give anybody the chance to even suspect discrimination against them on one of these grounds as it could land you in very hot water indeed. It is difficult to prove that you simply got a negative feeling about a person who claims that you deliberately refused him a house because of his skin colour or family status. To try and avoid these issues we have, in recent years, adopted a policy of not giving any tenant a decision at the viewing stage. If a person is interested in taking a place, his enthusiasm won't be dimmed by having to wait until the following day for a decision.

You are entitled, if you wish, not to let your property to those on social welfare, smokers, or people you are wary of. Many landlords are nervous of social welfare recipients, afraid they might be irresponsible. I don't have a problem with tenants who are in receipt of welfare. Neither do I understand why some landlords do. As long as the rent is paid on time, it is the tenant's business how he comes up with the money. (You can, in some health board areas, make it part of the deal that the payments, usually referred to as 'rent allowance', are made directly to you, the landlord, or into your bank account.)

There is really only one situation where you have to worry about how the rent is paid. It is not unknown for rented apartments to be used as brothels or drug supermarkets. If you suspect that this type of illegal activity is being carried out in your apartment then you should report your suspicions immediately to the gardaí. Quite apart from any moral or social obligations a landlord might feel in such a situation, he could also be found negligent in law. If for no other reason than this, take great care when choosing tenants.

Use your judgement – engage the potential tenant in conversation and interview him, when he is viewing the property, to get some idea what he is like. Be wary if he fudges on specifics like the name of his current landlord or employer. Don't be afraid to follow your instincts, but don't be surprised if, later, you discover that you got someone totally wrong. I once let a house to a lovely family. Everything seemed to be in order. Their references checked out, 50 per cent of the deposit and rent were paid in advance, the rest to be paid the following day. They had their granny with them when they viewed the place, the sort of thing which is calculated to inspire trust. Even our plumber, a man not easily impressed, sang their praises when he called to install a washing machine. 'Such a nice family,' he said, 'with such well-mannered children.' Having tricked their way into the house paying only half of the deposit, they never paid another penny and were always out or more likely not answering the door, when we called. It took three months to get them out. Thankfully, I have more often been surprised by people who turned out better than expected. Let's face it, in an ideal world we would never let anything to anybody we were less than 100 per cent happy with. In the real world, however, there is always a balance to be struck between letting a place quickly and getting an ideal tenant. Nobody gets it right all of the time. Often the people I have taken a chance on have been the very ones who turned out best.

Only two absolute rules govern my choice of tenant. One is that I won't let to anyone who tries to beat me down on price. People who begin by trying to negotiate a better deal for themselves will probably expect to continue in that way for the duration of the tenancy and will eventually wear you down. It sends out all of the wrong signals, starting with the shoe on the wrong foot, you might say, to give the tenant the upper hand when it comes to the rent. My other absolute, no, no is letting to relatives or friends. I am sure that there are, out there, hundreds of examples of people for whom letting to their friends proved very successful, and good luck to them, but I know that I couldn't work it. Any friend or relative is welcome to *'borrow'* a place anytime, if they need it and it's available. I have no problem with that, but it's the combination of friendship and money that I would find hard to manage.

THE LEASE

Before taking the letting to the next stage, you must make the terms of the agreement crystal clear to the tenant. Like most other aspects of the process it is best to put in writing what has been agreed between you. Make out a checklist, similar to the one below and fill the spaces as you go. We write it in a duplicate notebook and hand a copy to the tenant. (Ready-made leases are available from the IPOA. See page 202 for address.)

Address of property:	55 Richmond Avenue, Cork
Rent:	€800 monthly
Deposit:	€800 (Paid)
Term:	Six months
Commencement date:	13 July 2004
No. of people to occupy the premises:	4
Services included in the rent:	None
Refuse collection:	Paid by tenant
Pets:	Not Allowed
Smoking:	Allowed

You may wish to include other items about which you have definite views. The aim is to eliminate future disagreement and to work out the details which will form part of the letting agreement. One month's rent is the usual amount taken by landlords as a deposit against accidental or malicious damage. Depending on whether the rent is paid weekly or monthly, collect, in addition, a week's or a month's rent. Expect to be told a great range of stories about why it is difficult to come up with the deposit just now, even though normally there would be no problem. They will, of course, have it without fail next week. Discount all such sob stories and send the good ones to me – I'm making a collection. If someone is a good prospect they will find the deposit. If someone's friends or family won't help him out, if necessary, with a deposit then why should you, a complete stranger, offer him an interest-free loan?

In the past it was common practice to let properties on a casual basis. Young people moved in and out of flats willy nilly, often without thinking to inform the landlord that a change of tenants had taken place. Tenants were plentiful and easygoing and as long as the rent was on the table every Friday night everyone was happy. Alas, times have changed. Letting, like every other aspect of life has become more regulated, for better or worse. There is certainly protection for both sides in having a contract which clearly states the obligations of each party to the other. Details of the rent, the term, the commencement date and the deposit will obviously be included. Other terms usually include some or all of the following.

The Tenant
- Tenancy begins when the tenant receives the keys of the house or apartment. The deposit is held by the landlord against any damages or failure to keep to the terms of this agreement. The landlord is entitled to retain the deposit if the property is not kept in reasonable condition. If it is not left clean and tidy the cost of cleaning will be deducted.
- Deposits are refunded, subject to the above conditions, after the tenant has vacated the property and surrendered the keys and the landlord has had time to thoroughly inspect the premises. The deposit can *never* be used in lieu of the last month's rent.
- Rent must always be paid in full on the due date.
- The tenant agrees to use the property as a private residence only.

- Any defects in the apartment/house or any repairs found necessary must be brought to the attention of the landlord by the tenant within one week of occupancy.
- All furniture, fittings and appliances supplied are deemed to be acceptable to the tenant unless an express agreement to the contrary is made before the commencement of the tenancy. These items must be left in situ. The tenant, at his own expense, may substitute them, however, with the landlord's agreement, during the tenancy, with items of equal value. (Tenants sometimes do this if they don't like the landlord's taste.) These items must then be allowed to remain in the apartment/house at the end of the tenancy.
- The tenant agrees to notify the landlord immediately of any repairs that may become necessary and for which the landlord is responsible under this agreement.
- The landlord will be given reasonable access to all areas of the property whenever required to carry out all necessary and desirable repairs.
- The tenant shall not hold the landlord responsible for any loss or theft of his goods. The tenant must, himself, insure personal items if he so wishes.
- Any unacceptable noise levels or disturbance to neighbouring tenants or residents will render the contract null and void and will result in termination of the tenancy.
- The tenant agrees to transfer all utilities – telephone, electricity and gas – into tenant's own name and discharge all bills for same unless other arrangements are agreed with the landlord.
- The tenant will be liable for all service charges levied on the premises by the local authority for the entire duration of this agreement.
- The tenant shall not sublet part or all of the premises without written permission.
- The tenant will not allow any more than _____ persons to reside or otherwise occupy the premises during the course of the tenancy.
- The tenant agrees not to keep any animals on the premises.

Many landlords insist on 12-month leases but we have found them increasingly difficult to get as people are becoming more and more mobile. Notice, in writing, is required if the tenant is leaving or if the landlord wishes to reoccupy the premises. In practice, this notice is rarely given in writing and usually this poses no problem. Make sure, however, that when your tenant gives notice you get a definite date when he or she is moving out. A shifting vacating date will leave you unsure of where you stand. Sometimes it makes no difference to you when the tenant moves out, but the chances are that he will finally leave just when you are about to go on holiday or you are unavailable for other reasons.

The Landlord
The landlord agrees:

- to allow the tenant quiet enjoyment of the premises. The tenant is paying for a home and his privacy must not be violated; and
- to maintain and keep in good order both the exterior and interior of the building and its surrounding area.

An inventory of all furniture, fittings and appliances will also form part of the contract and should be checked and signed separately by both parties. See page 124 for a typical inventory.

SUGGESTED HOUSE RULES
If your property is in multiple units, it would be wise to make out a list of house rules and display them prominently. These rules could also form part of the contract. You might wish to add or take from the list below.

- Be aware of fire exits and do not cause any situation, which may put your life or the lives of others at risk.
- Leave rubbish in its designated area at all times and be aware of days when bins are emptied. It is the tenant's responsibility to place their rubbish in the bin provided.
- Do not obstruct common passageways with bicycles, prams, bags or furniture.
- Allow other people peace in their homes, come and go quietly.
- If there is a fault in electricity, gas or water installations or if you notice anything that might lead to a problem, let your landlord (or agent) know immediately.

- Close doors securely to avoid unwanted guests. Secure your own unit by closing doors, windows, etc. when you are out or asleep.
- If your flat is fitted with a fire/smoke detector, make sure you do not use open flames or allow items being cooked to burn as this will cause the smoke alarm to be activated.
- When rent is due, pay it on time and in full together with any charges for services. If you have a difficulty, discuss your problem with your landlord (or agent). It is much easier to handle a small problem early than leave it until disaster strikes.
- Do not allow strangers into the house. If you are not sure who a caller is, ask for ID.

GUIDELINES FOR THE TENANT

Our experiences over the years have shown that quite a number of young people (and indeed many not so young) lack many of the domestic skills earlier generations took for granted. Some time ago we decided to incorporate some guidelines for looking after the property into the agreement we use. As with the house rules above you might wish to alter them to fit your own situation.

- Kitchens should be kept clean at all times and all rubbish disposed of in the appropriate manner.
- Cookers should be cleaned at least weekly.
- Fridges must be kept clean and defrosted when necessary.
- Floors should be thoroughly swept daily.
- Drains should be kept free. Never put any solid matter such as food remains down the sink. The tenant will be billed for the cost of servicing the drains should they become blocked through misuse.
- Burn marks to furniture and worktops from hot pans, cigarettes and so on are regarded as damage and the cost of repairs will be deducted from the deposit.
- Carpets should be vacuumed at least every two weeks and kept free of stains and damage.
- Windows should be opened regularly especially during cooking and after using the shower.
- Curtains should be kept open during daylight hours. Net curtains should always hang properly.
- Beds must be kept clean and stain free. This applies especially where there are young children.

- All windows and doors should be secured. Electrical appliances, such as heaters and cookers, must be switched off when the tenant is absent from the premises.
- Redecoration of the apartment/house is not permitted without prior consultation.
- Nails or screws should not be driven into walls, furniture or doors.
- On leaving the property the tenant must ensure that it has been thoroughly cleaned, all rubbish has been removed and all utility bills, telephone/gas, etc., have been paid.

These measures will ensure that the tenant will have his/her deposit returned in full.

Though a novice landlord would be well advised to pay a visit to his solicitor to have the agreement drawn up and signed, a more experienced property owner might feel confident in using a ready-prepared contract, available in any legal stationers. Make sure the one you are offered complies with the 2004 Tenancies Act (see Chapter 11). Alternatively, a simpler contract can be typed up which notes the terms agreed by both parties. Rights granted to tenants under the 2004 law may not be contracted away, and as long as this does not happen, all agreements are valid and enforceable.

Checklist

Completed	Date
Interview	_____
References checked	_____
Deposits received	_____
Agreement signed	_____
Inventory checked	_____
Utilities arranged	_____
Keys and rent book handed over	_____

Chapter 11
Up and Running: Managing Your Business

YOUR SUPPORT TEAM

'*The secret of staying sane as a landlord*,' according to Fiona Fullerton, '*is to have a good back-up team and an organised filing system.*' Important though both of these are, I would argue that a sense of humour is the first essential. Consider the following exchange.

Tenant: There's a problem with my shower. The water isn't coming out properly.

Me: What do you mean, 'properly', could you be a bit more specific?

Tenant: Well, it's hard to explain, but when I turn it on it sort goes sideways and hits the shower door and it's very awkward having to bend over to the side to wash.

Me (mystified): I suppose I'd better send out the plumber to have a look. (After a pause and a dropped penny) Have you tried moving the showerhead to redirect the flow?

Tenant: Oh! Can you do that? I didn't know. Thanks.

I kid you not, this actually happened. After the ability to laugh at the vagaries, a list of reliable tradespersons is an absolute necessity. You need:

- a plumber – one who is registered with Bord Gáis if you have gas in the house;

- an electrician with a RECI certificate;
- a man-Friday with the willingness and the ability to do odd jobs such as fixing locks and tidying up gardens;
- a *man* with a van (let's not be too politically correct) who will shift furniture and dump large amounts of rubbish when required; and
- a cleaner, good ones are like gold.

You will build your team over time. When you find good people treat them well and they will be there when you need them. If, for any reason, relations become sour with any of your support team then move on and find someone else. Ask your friends to recommend people. Use the local paper if necessary, but use it to make contacts before you need them. Try to avoid looking for someone new in an emergency.

Picture the scene! You are in Killarney (or Barcelona or Prague) for the weekend and you get a call from your tenants telling you that a pipe has burst. There's water everywhere and they don't know what to do. If you don't have a regular plumber trying to find one in this situation is, to say the least, difficult and you don't need that kind of stress when you're on holiday.

If you have spent hours looking for things once too often, you will probably have devised some system for keeping papers. Ideally, each piece of paper should be neatly filed away as soon as it is generated. In this way a disorganised mess is never created in the first place and any particular receipt or letter can be found quickly, and with a minimum of fuss. If you consider it unrealistic to file each piece of paper as it comes in then at least get a box or a folder and put everything into it until you have the time to deal with it.

LEGAL FRAMEWORK OF LANDLORD–TENANT LAW

If you ask any landlord what his greatest fear is, he will probably tell you that it's the tenant from hell. This is the tenant who is anti-social, dirty, plays his music at a deafening volume, upsetting neighbours or other tenants, and breaks everything he touches. He won't pay rent and won't move out. Thankfully, such tenants are extremely rare as most live in constant fear of not getting their deposit back. For many, that deposit represents their only chance to get another place when necessary. It is often, in effect, their only security against homelessness. To allay fears on both sides a huge body of law exists to regulate landlord–tenant relations and all landlords should know the fundamentals of that law. Solicitors and other professionals will always be necessary, but a little knowledge of the law can help us to ask them the right questions and to decode their answers. A working knowledge of the relevant law can also be a great contribution to peace of mind. At the very least, if you're informed about the rights and obligations of both tenant and landlord, you're less likely to dig a hole for yourself through either innocence or ignorance.

Up to about the late seventies, landlord–tenant relations had been governed largely by custom, precedent and outmoded legislation. In 1980 the Landlord and Tenant (Amendment) Act was the first attempt to bring a modern legal framework to bear on this relationship.

In the nineties a number of measures were passed in order to improve the condition of private rented accommodation and regulate the provision of this accommodation by landlords.

Rent Books

The Housing (Miscellaneous Provisions) Act of 1992 included the following provisions on rent books.

- The landlord must supply a rent book to the tenant within one month of the commencement of the tenancy.
- The rent book must contain the following details:
  - the name of the tenant and the address of the premises;
  - the name and address of the landlord;
  - details of the amount of rent and when and how it is payable;
  - a receipt for all rent paid;
  - details of any payments made to the landlord for services such as electricity and gas;
  - the date of commencement of the tenancy, the terms such as the length, e.g. six months, and the notice required; and
  - the amount of the deposit and the conditions on which the deposit is repayable.
- All changes, such as an increase in rent must be recorded in the rent book.

In addition to the above, the following points should also be considered.

- Each tenant must be provided with a full inventory of all furniture, fittings and appliances in the accommodation.
- Each time that rent or other payments for services are made by the tenant, the payment must be recorded and signed for by the landlord or his agent. When payments are made other than in person, such as by standing order, they must be recorded in the rent book within three months.
- The tenant retains the rent book and the landlord may have access to it to record payments and make changes.
- Failure to provide a rent book carries a fine of up to €1,000.

Legal Minimum Standards

Another important milestone was reached when the set of regulations called '*The Standards for Rented Houses*' became law in 1993. Under this provision, certain minimum standards for rented property were laid down. Responsibility for the enforcement of these standards was vested in each local authority. In brief the standards are as follows.

- The premises must be in a proper state of structural repair, with roof, walls, ceilings, floors and stairs in good order.
- A sink, with hot and cold water, must be provided.
- A toilet and bath or shower facilities must be provided.
- Adequate means for heating, cooking and storage of food are essential.
- Installations for the supply of electricity or gas are to be kept in good repair and safe working order.
- Common areas must be well kept and in clean condition.
- A secure handrail must be provided for common stairways.
- Adequate ventilation must be provided in all bedrooms. Vents must be installed to maintain the circulation of air.
- Bathrooms and kitchens must have adequate ventilation.
- Baths and showers may be shared between flats, but must not be more than two floors above or below the flat in question.
- At least one toilet and one bath or shower must be provided for each two units unless there is only one person in each flat, in which case one bathroom is required for up to four flats.

Registration

In addition to provisions re rent books and standards, a 1996 act required that landlords register the tenancies of rented dwellings with the local authority in whose area the dwelling is situated, within one month of the letting. This registration system has now been superseded by the new regulations contained in the Residential Tenancies Act (2004).

It is vitally important that landlords familiarise themselves with the law in matters such as registration and minimum standards. The provisions outlined above are mandatory requirements. To carry out our business in a professional manner, we have a duty to our tenants to go beyond these minimum basic standards and provide the best possible accommodation. Tenants are our customers and our business will thrive if they are satisfied.

PROPOSED NEW LEGISLATION

The Residential Tenancies Act means substantial changes to the current rights and obligations of both tenants and landlords. To provide for greater security of tenure and to establish a speedy, inexpensive and effective mechanism for dispute resolution, the government, in 1999, set up a commission to examine the issues and make recommendations to achieve these aims. The findings of this board became the basis of the new legislation, which came into effect in September 2004.

The main features of the new law are as follows.

Security of Tenure

The bill provides for a significant degree of security of tenure. After six months a tenant will have an automatic right to a four-year lease independent of the terms of the existing agreement. During the first six months of a tenancy, the landlord will be free to terminate the agreement, no reason given. For the next three and a half years termination is possible only in limited circumstances, such as the landlord wanting to sell the property, substantially renovate, change the use of the premises, live in it himself or let it to a member of his own family. If the accommodation is no longer suitable for the needs of the occupier, for example, the number of bed spaces is no longer adequate, the contract may be terminated.

Termination notice, which applies to tenants as well as landlords, is on a sliding scale, from 28 days within the initial six-month period, rising to 112 days after four years. If the tenant breaks his obligations and fails to remedy the breach, the period of notice required will be 28 days, regardless of the duration of the tenancy. During his four-year lease, a tenant who wishes to be released from his contract may seek permission to sublet. The landlord may refuse permission, but the tenant may then terminate the tenancy.

Anti-social behaviour on the part of tenant is clearly defined for the first time and will incur a seven-day notice to quit. Arrears of 28 days or abandoning the property will also mean forfeiture of tenancy. If a single tenant in a multiple tenancy, does damage and other tenants fail to co-operate with the landlord in his censure they too can be asked to forfeit their tenancy. In addition, the landlord has an obligation to deal with anti-social behaviour on the part of his tenant so that others are not unduly affected by it.

The Private Residential Tenancies Board (PRTB)

The PRTB, established on a pilot basis since November 2003, and on a permanent basis by the new law, has a number of functions. These are as follows.

Registration of Tenancies

The new registration system replaces the largely unworkable 1996 system. Landlords will be required to register the commencement and termination of each tenancy with the PRTB and to pay a registration fee of €70 per tenancy. A composite fee of €300 will apply to buildings containing four or more units registered at the same time. A considerable amount of detail is sought including names, addresses and PPS numbers of the owner and of each tenant. Registration must be completed within one month of a new tenancy or it will attract a double fee. Non-registration is not an offence until a final warning is issued by the PRTB. Once registered, the landlord is obliged to notify the board every time the rent changes. It is an offence to supply false information to the board.

Provision of Information and Advice

The PRTB will engage in research and monitoring of the rental market in order to be in a position to advise all interested parties and to aid it in dispute resolution. It also makes best practice guides and model leases available to registered landlords.

Dispute Resolution

At the time of writing, the board is in its infancy, but it is envisaged that the PRTB will replace the current role of the courts when disputes occur. Issues such as the refund of deposits, up to now dealt with by the Small Claims Court, breaches of tenancy obligations and cases of rent arrears are within the remit of the board. A two-stage process is in place involving (a) mediation or adjudication, and (b) a public hearing before a tribunal which may be appealed to the High Court, though only on a point of law.

The board will have the power to increase or decrease rents which they feel are not in line with current market levels. Rent reviews are not permitted more than once a year. Among the changes in the obligations of landlords and tenants are those relating to mainten-ance. Up to now, under the terms of the standard letting agreement, tenants were responsible for maintaining the interior of the property in good order. Landlords are now required to maintain the interior as well as the structure to the standard that applied at the commencement of the letting. The tenant may not substantially alter the premises, though he may redecorate, and he has a responsibility to make good any damage that has occurred during the course of his tenancy.

LOOKING AFTER YOUR TENANT

At the risk of sounding like a Victorian nanny, telling you what's good for you, I want to remind you that your tenants are your customers, not your friends. Forget this and you may regret it. Many of the problems landlords and tenants have with each other have been caused by neglecting to maintain proper interpersonal boundaries. Make it clear at the outset what is expected and what tenants can expect in return. Make sure you carry out your side of the deal to the letter and there is a much greater chance of the tenant doing likewise. The second essential is to have a good knowledge of the rights and obligations of both parties. Go back to your letting agreement if you are unsure. If a problem needs to be tackled then do so with the facts clearly in your mind. Be understanding and kind, but firm. In other words, be professional in your approach. Another aspect of this professional approach is maintaining good practice by providing rent books, keeping them up to date and dealing promptly with tenants' queries.

If your tenant is in arrears, your first enquiry is to ascertain the reason. People often lose their jobs through no fault of their own or they become ill. A person, who has been a good tenant up to now, may at least be given the benefit of the doubt. Perhaps the answer is an application for rent allowance to tide him over. You have to decide whether to charge the full rent or waive some or all of it for a while. Sometimes it's in your own best interest to take a loss for a while if the tenant has a good record.

So what *do* you do about the tenant from hell mentioned earlier, the one who won't pay and won't leave? First, be very careful not to put yourself in the wrong. Under no circumstances can you throw him and all his belongings out on the street, however tempted or justified you might be. You run the risk of being accused of theft or assault if you take the law into your own hands, besides which due legal process must be adhered to. Your recourse in extreme situations is to the PRTB which has injunctive powers in certain circumstances. Do not be tempted to speed up the eviction process by having the utilities, such as water and electricity, cut off. This may be seen as harassment, even though these accounts may be in your name and you may in fact be paying the tenant's bills. Once you have applied to the PRTB and begin the legal process do not discuss the matter with the tenant. He may try blackmail, offer to leave if you give him money, or try a hard-luck story. Discussion only clouds the issues. Your best bet is to stick to your guns because, if he realises that you mean business, he may just up sticks and disappear.

In all my years as a landlord I have only been in this position once and in that case the tenants left once the legal process was set in motion. Such people don't usually have a grand evil intent, that's much too romantic. Neither are they out to get you. They are usually just desperate individuals whose lives are a mess. They are often in enough trouble already and won't stick around for more.

Fire Safety
Fire Safety must not be overlooked when considering a landlord's obligations to his tenants. Taking the right precautions can, literally, mean the difference between life and death.

Legislation relating to fire safety in residential buildings is contained in the Fire Services Act 1981, and the Building Control Act 1990. If you are letting either a house as a single unit, or a custom-built modern apartment, fire regulations need not worry you unduly. As a condition of planning permission, apartments must be built to a very high fire safety standard. Houses have the advantage of being separated from the surrounding dwellings, so that the risk of fire spreading to engulf several units is small. As part of a landlord's duty of care to his tenants, however, he should asses his house or apartment to eliminate any hazards. Smoke alarms, if not already installed, are simple to fix to ceilings – one near the kitchen, one in the hallway and one on the landing would be sufficient for most homes. A small fire extinguisher and a fire blanket near the cooking area would complete a reasonable fire safety kit. In addition tenants should be encouraged to plan an escape drill incorporating:

- escape routes to evacuate the property;
- *one* meeting place outside the property;
- the closing of all doors as occupants leave; and
- the acknowledgment that the property should not be re-entered for any reason.

Fire Safety in Flats

My insurance broker tells me that flats are the single biggest fire risk in terms of accommodation. An excellent, if highly technical, guide called *Fire Safety in Flats* is produced by the Department of the Environment and if you ring them they will send you a copy free of charge.

The 1981 Fire Services Act places a statutory responsibility on persons having control over residential premises to take all reasonable precautions to guard against fire. This duty is shared by the owner, the tenant, the manager, the caretaker, visitors, maintenance people, etc. The 1991 Building Regulations set out the requirements including fire safety standards for certain buildings. These regulations cover design and construction of new buildings and recommendations on fire safety management within existing buildings converted into flats prior to 1991. Some of these recommendations can be implemented immediately with little or no expense, while others should form part of a planned implementation within as short a timescale as possible.

Principles of Fire Safety

The principles of fire safety are:

- the avoidance of an outbreak of fire;
- the provision of escape routes to enable occupants to leave the building safely should a fire occur;

- the early detection and early warning of fire within the building;
- the limitation of the development and spread of a fire;
- the containment of the fire and smoke in the area where an outbreak occurs; and
- the management of fire safety.

If you were to take only one single measure in a bid to prevent fires it would have to be the installation of smoke alarms. Ideally, this would be part of a complete fire detection, alarm and emergency lighting system, but the simple, battery-operated, stand-alone alarm is incomparably better than nothing at all.

Thought should also be given to furnishings. Upholstered furniture should be resistant to ignition from a cigarette for example. Curtains should not be near the cooker, rubbish should be carefully stored so as not to be a hazard. Don't forget to have all electrical and gas installations checked regularly. Some tenants have an unfortunate tendency to fancy themselves as DIY experts, even to the extent of messing around with the plumbing and electrics. While a leak in the plumbing can do a huge amount of damage, it is unlikely to cause loss of life. Electricity, on the other hand, can present a real danger if misused. Our electrician has a watching brief. Any time he is called out to a property, whatever the reason, he does a check around to make sure all is as it should be.

As a landlord it is wise to bear in mind that tenants, especially the young and inexperienced, need reminding of the dangers of fire. Be specific. A general admonition is pointless. Point out any possible fire hazards within the flat, such as putting clothes on or too near radiators. Point out the importance of such things as cleaning the filter in the tumble dryer, a cause of many fires as it can ignite if it gets too hot. Your tenants may, at the very least, appreciate your concern for their safety.

It is a good idea to place prohibitory notices reminding tenants not to obstruct escape routes. No upholstered furniture should be left in hallways or corridors. Ensure all doors are easily opened and that mats and rugs do not present a trip hazard.

Fire doors throughout the flat (except for the bathroom door) are a critical part of fire defence as are windows with openings of not less than about 1 square metre. Make sure there are no bars or grills on the windows. Work out, in conjunction with each tenant as soon as he moves into the flat, the best possible escape route. The most effective escape is usually by way of a fire-protected entrance hall where no likely source of fire exists, but do not overlook the usefulness of flat roofs as exits in the event of an outbreak.

While the building specifications, as they relate to fire prevention, are outside the scope of this book and should be discussed with a qualified fire engineer, it is worth a landlord's while to be aware of the principles involved. Current thinking mainly focuses on the importance of protected escape routes and containment of fire. In existing buildings double slabbed ceilings, fire doors and lobbies inside the main door of the flat are all recommended in addition to the large window openings mentioned above.

TAX, INSURANCE AND SERVICE CHARGES
Income tax and PRSI are payable on all rental income. This is what makes properties which offer tax concessions on income seem attractive (see Chapter 9).

In the past landlords had the reputation of being experts at tax evasion. True or not, things have changed for the better in this area. Most landlords now realise that it makes little sense to hide or underdeclare tax liabilities. Apart from the fact that you run a very high risk of being caught and attracting extremely high penalties and interest, often a multiple of the tax owed in the first place, you cannot use your profits to expand your business.

Each year you must prepare an account for each rented property and submit it to the Revenue Commissioners. An accountant will prepare this for you if you wish, but unless you are operating as a limited company you may submit your own figures. Tax officials are very helpful to callers and will go out of their way to advise you if you ring them with a query.

Refurbishment Relief
If you have purchased, for residential letting, a property in need of refurbishment, a special tax relief is available. Allowable expenditure includes money spent on reconstruction and repair. The work must comply with certain guidelines issued by the Department of the Environment, Housing & Local Government. Qualifying expenditure is allowable over eight years against all rental income, not just the rent from the property in question. Unlike other tax-discounted

property, if it is sold, or ceases to be let, the tax relief is not transferable.

Calculating Your Tax

In order to calculate the amount of tax due on your rent, you must first get into the habit of keeping every slip of paper connected with the property. Most important are receipts for things you buy, such as electrical appliances, and services you pay for, such as plumbing. These can be deducted from the income. If you have more than one property write on each receipt which property it applies to and keep a box or folder for that property. (This is also a good way of keeping records for the purposes of guarantees and warranties.)

Begin by calculating your gross rental income. Don't rely on memory to do this. Rent should, each week or month, depending on how often it is paid, be entered into a ledger. If you are computer literate a number of programmes are available to make keeping accounts an easy matter. Sage and Quick Books are popular. Calculate how much rent was actually received in the previous year – from 1 January to 31 December.

Expenditure allowable against tax due includes:

- utilities (gas, electricity) and service charges;
- refurbishment relief as explained above;
- special tax relief, e.g. Section 23 which allows a tax write-off for the capital cost of the property (see Chapter 9);
- mortgage interest;
- mortgage insurance;
- buildings and contents insurance;
- service charges;
- repairs and maintenance;
- management or rent collection expenses;
- capital expenditure qualifies for a tax write-off over eight years. This applies to furniture, appliances and other items such as flooring, sanitary ware, and so on.

Having deducted these items from the gross rent, you arrive at the net figure on which tax will be calculated. It may be a minus figure, in which case you have made a loss. This loss can be carried forward to subsequent years and offset against future profits. If you do have a profit this will be added to any other income you have. Tax and PRSI will then be collected from your entire income. For properties within the State, losses on one property can be offset against profits on another. The Revenue Commissioners now operate a self-assessment system which means that you are obliged to make tax returns and to submit payment in full without being billed.

Insurance
In the years since the 9/11 attacks, the price of property insurance has skyrocketed. Nobody seems able to explain why. The New York disaster is cited as a reason by the insurance companies, but premiums in New York itself have, it seems, been largely unaffected. Whatever the reason, expect to pay a substantial amount to insure your property. A number of factors need to be taken into account.

- Do not underinsure. All policies have, in the small print, what is called, the *'average clause'*. What this means is that, if you are underinsured and something happens, you will not be fully compensated. In effect, if you are deemed to have valued the property at, say, half the true value and, as a result, paid only half the correct premium, then you will be allowed only half of any justifiable claim you make.
- Do not overinsure, as the *'average clause'* does not work in reverse. Your money is completely wasted.
- Watch house price inflation. Adjust your valuations as prices rise.
- Calculate the correct premium by taking the market value of the property and deducting the cost of the site, as this is not insurable. Consider the cost of replacing the building should it be destroyed by fire, for example. An engineer, quantity surveyor or a competent builder can give an indication of the replacement cost of a building at so much per square metre. Having calculated the ground floor area of the building and multiplied by the number of storeys, use this figure to calculate the replacement cost.
- Don't make the mistake of thinking you don't need to insure the house contents if you are letting an unfurnished property, or if you think they are of little value. A much more important consideration than the value of a few sticks of furniture is the public liability element included in each policy. This is your only

safeguard if a tenant has an accident such as a fall on a loose piece of carpet.

- Install security items such as deadlocks on external doors and window locks and smoke alarms. Not only will they protect your tenants and your property, but you may get a discount on your insurance premium.

Refuse Collection Charges

Charges imposed by local authorities vary considerably from one area to another. As the law currently stands the occupier (tenant) of a single-unit rented dwelling, such as a house or apartment, is responsible for payment. In a multiple-unit property, the onus is on the landlord to pay the service charges. This seems straightforward enough, except that some authorities appear to have a policy of making the landlord pay collection charges for any property where the tenant shirks his responsibility, especially if he leaves without paying. As the situation is somewhat confused, it might be a good idea to levy each tenant with a monthly payment to cover the charge and then look after the actual payment yourself.

Stamp Duty on Letting Agreements

Most residential letting agreements are exempt from stamp duty. Unless the term exceeds 35 years or the annual rent is over €19,050 stamp duty need not be a concern. The rate, where it applies, is 1 per cent of the *total* annual rent (not 1 per cent of the marginal amount). A further €12.50 is payable if there is a rent review clause in the agreement. Each official copy of the lease also incurs the same, €12.50 charge.

> **Remember**
> When in any doubt about legal and financial issues, it's always better to consult your advisers. It is better to be safe than sorry.

CAPITAL GAINS TAX AND CAPITAL ACQUISITIONS TAX

Capital Gains Tax (CGT) is a tax on the profit made when property is sold or otherwise disposed of, such as by way of a gift. All costs associated with the sale, such as solicitor's and auctioneer's fees, are fully allowable against this tax. The amount initially paid for the property, all costs associated with the purchase, including stamp duty, legal fees and any money spent on refurbishment and improvement can also be deducted from the sale price to calculate the capital gain on which the tax is paid (assuming or course this expenditure has not been allowed already against income tax on rent). Inflation in property prices is no longer allowed, but an annual exemption which currently stands at €1,270 can be claimed. The current rate of CGT is 20 per cent.

While all of this sounds very technical it is not as complicated as it seems. Also your solicitor or estate agent will have a ready-reckoner which will give an instant right answer to the arithmetic.

Capital Acquisitions Tax (CAT) is similar to CGT. It is the tax which applies when property passes from one family member to another – though no tax is due on transfers between a husband and wife. Tax is, however, payable on transfers to children. Each child is entitled to inherit, or receive as a gift, €441,198 including property, free of tax. In order to avoid CAT some people buy properties in their children's names. Trusts may also be set up to reduce liability. A trust works by bypassing the beneficiary as far as ownership is concerned. In other words the beneficiaries, usually the inheritors, of the wealth have the benefit of the funds and property in their lifetimes without actually owning them, thus avoiding CAT.

The family home is exempt from CAT if the inheritor has lived in it for three years prior to the inheritance.

A FINAL WORD ON THE RESIDENTIAL TENANCIES ACT 2004

The government-appointed Commission on the Private Residential Rented Sector had as its brief to investigate the entire industry and to make recommendations which would lead to an increase and improvement in the supply of residential accommodation. At its launch the minister indicated that the function of the commission was to '*enable the private rented sector to develop its maximum potential and be seen as an option of choice rather than a tenure of transition before home ownership or social housing*'. It was stressed that any recommendations made should be '*appropriate, fair and workable*'.

The landlords' organisation, The Irish Property Owners Association (IPOA), despite being represented on the commission by its chairman, Stephen Faughnan, has been vociferous in its criticism of the new legislation which was drafted on the basis of the commission's findings. '*We would have been quite happy if the recommendations of the commission had been implemented but subsequent amendments have altered the entire balance in favour of the tenant,*' Faughnan has said. '*This will make investing in residential property less attractive for investors, the opposite of what the commission set out to achieve.*'

Fintan McNamara, Press Officer of the IPOA, believes that the spirit of the legislation is very anti-landlord and could create a climate of suspicion between landlord and tenant.

The IPOA commissioned its own survey of the rental sector in 2002 and the results make interesting reading.

- Regarding the type of lease which is most common, 57 per cent of tenants reported having a written agreement and 30 per cent, a satisfactory verbal one.
- The vast majority of tenants, 92 per cent, reported the quality of their relationship with their landlord or his representative as either '*casual and friendly*' or '*business-like*'.
- When asked about the Residential Tenancies Board, only 45 per cent saw it as having a valuable role in dispute resolution.
- Regarding changes in the rules on security of tenure, 53 per cent of respondents said it would have no effect on them, given their circumstances.

This suggests that current practice in private renting is far more satisfactory than anyone thought. The tenants' organisation, Threshold, would not agree with the views of the IPOA. For years they have campaigned on the issue of security of tenure. Renting, they say, should be a viable option to meet the long-term needs of a family. They feel that the act does not go far enough and are unhappy that a landlord may still evict a tenant to suit his own convenience.

As with all such issues, it is difficult to get the balance right between opposing viewpoints.

Chapter 12
For the Tenant

This chapter has been included because the book would not be complete without it. Letting cannot take place without people wishing to rent. I hope those readers who are property owners will not skip it but will read it to try to understand how the market looks from the renter's perspective. Besides, landlords and tenants are not mutually exclusive groups. People often alternate between both camps several times during their lives.

In the early nineties, driving through traditional flatland areas of an evening, the scramble for a half-decent place to live was evident in the queues of 10 or even 20 people lined up on the footpaths waiting to view flats. In a climate where accommodation was in such short supply, there was little incentive for landlords to maintain even basic standards of hygiene and comfort in their properties. We may, however, be beginning to feel the winds of change. The building industry seems, at last, to be getting its act together and has significantly increased the number of residential units coming on the market. The year 2003 saw over 63,000 completions nationwide, the largest number ever built in one year and 2004 has continued this trend. There is also some evidence that rents have softened a little as pressure has eased though this may only be temporary.

FINDING A PLACE TO RENT
The obvious place to start looking for a place to rent is the local evening paper in the area in which you wish to live. Ring several

numbers from the classified ads initially, just to get an idea of how much you will need to pay for what you want. If you are a student or if you work in a large workplace study the notice boards in your college or company. Post your own notice stating your needs as there are always people looking to share or sublet. In larger colleges students may have access to an accommodation office where dedicated staff will point them in the right direction and give advice on what to expect.

It is a good idea to prepare a checklist in advance. Then when you view a place you can tick off the facilities available. It's surprising how quickly you forget what you have seen, making comparisons difficult.

When you make an appointment with a landlord to view a property there are certain realities you should keep in mind. First, many properties, especially the better ones, are snapped up quickly. This means that if you find a place that suits your needs you must be prepared to make a decision and act immediately. There really is little point in looking at every available property, wasting an inordinate amount of time as most of them will be let while you are dithering. Renting is still, for most people, a relatively short-term accommodation solution, so don't hang about waiting for your dream home to come on the letting market. Think in practical terms.

- Is the area near your work or college?
- Are there good transport links?
- Is it a safe area?
- Are there facilities you need – pubs, restaurants, a library, a cinema and shops – nearby or within a short distance?
- Is the accommodation large enough for your needs?
- Does it have adequate furniture and a range of mod cons? You should expect a washing machine, a fridge-freezer, a microwave and a shower as standard. A drier and a dishwasher you can regard as luxuries.
- Is it dry or are there signs of damp like mould spots on walls and a musty smell?
- Are there safety features in the building? Smoke alarms, emergency lighting and the absence of bars on the windows may not seem very important now, but in the event of a fire they can literally be a matter of life or death.
- Who else lives in the building? Are they likely to be good neighbours?

Acting immediately means securing the accommodation by placing a booking deposit with the landlord. About €50 should be sufficient at this stage – enough to demonstrate that your interest is genuine. Have at least two references to hand, one from an employer and one personal, perhaps from your current landlord if you have one. Ideally, give a bank reference as well. Do not part with any more money than you have to and get a receipt with at least the landlord's name and phone number on it. If you are dealing with an agent from a well-known company you have some security but if not be aware that the person you are dealing with may not in fact be genuine. I am always amazed at how trusting many tenants are when it comes to handing over their hard-earned cash.

I know of at least one case where a landlord let a place, in good faith, to a couple whose reference checked out and seemed to have everything in order. Picture his astonishment when, some days after the tenants had moved in, he received a call from the local gardaí. The couple apparently advertised the flat themselves, using their own mobile number and, posing as landlords, pocketed six full deposits of €1,000 each. They made off with the money, but not before they added insult to injury by arranging to meet each of their victims at the same time and place to hand over keys. Some people, it seems, have a very warped sense of humour.

RIGHTS AND OBLIGATIONS

Landlord–tenant law sets out clearly the obligations of each party to the other. In addition, any written or verbal agreement made between landlord and tenant is binding as long as it does not contravene the law, so it should not be entered into without due consideration. It is to your advantage to have everything in writing, minimising the opportunity for disputes and ensuring you get your deposit back at the end of the tenancy. Review carefully all the important conditions of the contract as it may include conditions you would find unacceptable, such as prohibitions on having guests or keeping pets. You need to fully understand your contract because it can be difficult to assert your rights if you have broken the terms of your tenancy, even inadvertently.

In essence, the duties of a tenant are to pay the rent in full and on time, to keep the place clean and not to be a nuisance to others. The landlord is obliged to keep the building in good order and repair. He is also obliged to respect his tenants' privacy. If he needs access to carry out repairs, he should arrange a suitable time to call. Ideally, common sense should prevail, but it is amazing how trivial matters can cause major disputes between people.

As a tenant you have a right to live peacefully, in a habitable dwelling which is proofed against cold and wet, and is clean, sanitary and structurally sound. If something needs attention, talk to your landlord, but remember *please* that he is not responsible for you if, for instance, you lock yourself out in the middle of the night. Neither is he responsible for any damage caused by you or others to the house or apartment while you are renting. Your rent covers only normal wear and tear. Anything else, broken windows or furniture, for example, will be covered by your deposit unless you make good the damage before the end of the tenancy.

You should be aware that if a dispute occurs, neither you nor the landlord is entitled to change the locks without the consent of the other. Keeping you out of your home, or cutting off electricity, water or gas thus making it impossible for you to stay, is generally regarded as harassment and need not be tolerated. Neither has your landlord the right to take any of your belongings, either in lieu of rent or to compensate him for damage. You, on the other hand, are not entitled to refuse to pay rent if you have a grievance. At most you can withhold your payments, putting them aside until the matter is settled, but be cautious not to put yourself in the wrong. Nobody is entitled to take the law into his own hands, whatever the dispute. Due process must be observed at all times.

THE DEPOSIT

Most landlords will expect a deposit of at least one week's or one month's rent. This sum is usually held by the landlord, or his agent, as security against unpaid rent or any other breach of the tenancy agreement. You may lose some or all of your deposit if:

- bills or rent are left unpaid;
- there is substantial damage, over and above normal wear and tear, to the property;
- the premises is very dirty and requires professional cleaning (this assumes it was reasonably clean when you began your tenancy);
- you leave before the term is up, or fail to give the agreed notice.

You could be held liable for the rent for the rest of the letting period even if you no longer live there. If you have a sufficient reason to leave however, such as a change of job, your landlord may agree to allow you to sublet to another tenant.

The amount of the deposit and the conditions under which it will be returned must be recorded in either the agreement or the rent book. No other issue gives rise to as many disputes as deposits. If all else fails such disagreements may be thrashed out by referring them to the Private Residential Tenancies Board. This involves mediation, arbitration or a tribunal hearing.

RENT BOOKS

The Housing (Miscellaneous Provisions) Act of 1992 made a significant improvement in the lot of tenants. For the first time, a rent book or a written agreement was mandatory for each letting, and the tenant was entitled to know the name and address of his landlord. This meant that, if necessary, legal action could be taken against him. Taking such action may seem like one of the fundamental rights of any tenant anywhere but prior to this legislation a landlord could often not be sued simply because he could not be found in order to serve him with legal papers. In addition to these details, the rent book or agreement should contain the following information.

- A receipt for all money paid to the landlord or his agent.
- The address of the property.
- The length of the tenancy.
- The amount of the rent.
- When and how rent is payable.
- Details of payments to be made to the landlord (or his agent) for services such as electricity and service charges.
- The amount of the deposit held by the landlord and the conditions under which it is repayable.
- Any changes in the original terms of the tenancy, such as rent increases.
- An inventory, signed by both landlord and tenant (see page 124 for a sample inventory).

If the rent is paid directly to the landlord's bank account, these payments must be recorded in the rent book at least every three months. Where there is a written agreement, there is no onus on the landlord to provide a rent book as well, however receipts must be given to the tenant within three months of payment.

CHANGES IN THE LAW

The thrust of legislative changes under the Residential Tenancies Act 2004 is towards increasing the security of the tenant and regulating the industry. Key features of this new law, which impact directly on the tenant are:

- security of tenure;
- maintenance of the premises; and
- dispute resolution.

Security of Tenure

The most fundamental and far-reaching of these changes undoubtedly relates to security of tenure. Each tenant now has an automatic right to a four-year lease after a six-month probationary period. This right is, however, subject to some restrictions. Within the four-year lease period, the property owner may take advantage of five break clauses to terminate the tenancy. He or she can give notice to quit for the following reasons.

- The property is to be sold.
- Renovation or refurbishment is planned.
- It is proposed to change the use of the property, e.g. to commercial units.
- The owner wishes to occupy the property or give it to a member of his family.
- The accommodation is no longer suitable for the needs of the tenant. This applies if, for example, the size of the tenant's family increases.

Notice is on a sliding scale, depending on how long the tenant has been living in the property, and can be anywhere from 28 to 112 days. The growing problem of anti-social behaviour in rented property, something which affects decent tenants even more than landlords, is clearly defined and such behaviour may warrant no more than a seven-day notice to quit.

The principle has been established that a tenant may sublet (i.e. pass the remainder of his tenancy on to someone else if he wants to move out). The tenant can simply leave, without penalty, if this permission is refused by the landlord.

Repair, Maintenance and Redecoration

On the question of the upkeep of the property, the position, broadly speaking, up to the new act was that the exterior of the property and the structure of the building were the responsibility of the landlord and it was up to the tenant to keep the interior in good order and repair. Under the new law, the owner has a responsibility to keep the property inside and out at the same level of repair and decoration which pertained at the commencement of the tenancy. The tenant is entitled to redecorate to his own taste, but consultation with the landlord is advisable as this right is not clearcut.

Dispute Resolution

A new body, the Private Residential Tenancies Board (PRTB) has been set up to deal with serious disputes. It aims to be a cheap, readily available mechanism for dispute resolution.

When setting up the PRTB on a pilot basis in the Dublin area in 2003, the then Minister for Environment, Housing & Local Government, Martin Cullen, saw it as, *'An opportunity to remove the aggression and conflict that has so often marked disputes between landlords and tenants.'*

In order to avail of the PRTB mediation service when a dispute exists you should follow the steps given below.

- Contact the PRTB at Canal House, Canal Road, Dublin 6 (telephone (01) 888 2960).
- An information sheet will be sent out to you with an application form for completion by both landlord and tenant.
- When the completed application form has been received, the PRTB will make contact with both parties to confirm their agreement to mediation and to request all relevant documentation. The aim of mediation which is informal, local and confidential, is to assist both parties to help themselves tease

out the issues involved. Adjudication, the second stage, is binding though there is provision for appeal to the tribunal. At the appeal stage, a formal, public hearing will take place and a legally binding determination will be made. Further appeal is to the High Court, but only on a point of law.

RENT ALLOWANCE

People whose incomes are low may be entitled to a Supplementary Welfare Allowance. Under this scheme local health boards pay a subsidy towards the cost of private rented accommodation for those who qualify. Entitlement for this payment arises from the statutory obligation imposed on the health boards to provide accommodation for the homeless. While it was originally intended as a short-term, stop-gap measure, it has become for many, the only possible means of funding their accommodation. Where local authorities have failed for decades to provide sufficient housing for those on their waiting lists, it is difficult to see an alternative to the present system.

Local variations in the operation of the scheme exist but generally each tenant who qualifies must pay a minimum of (at the time of writing) €13 towards the cost of the rent, the balance being funded by the health board. The maximum payment is based on the individual's means and number of dependents. Payment may be made directly to the landlord or into his bank account. Recent cutbacks have meant a tightening up of the rules, so rent allowance may be more difficult to secure than in the past.

TAX CREDITS ON RENT

If you are employed and live in rented accommodation you are legally entitled to tax credits on the rent you have paid. These credits will appear in your annual tax credit allowance form (P2). In order to claim rent relief you need a special form available from your local tax office or the Revenue Commissioners. To complete the form the following information is required:

- your PPS number;
- your landlord's PPS number;
- your employer's name and address; and
- your letting agent's name and address (if relevant).

In addition you should forward to the tax office receipts for all rents paid (keep copies). If you have any queries you can contact your local tax office.

Remember
As a tenant it is in your best interest to know both your rights and your obligations.

Chapter 13
Investing Abroad

Lying on a beach in beautiful Nerja, on Spain's Costa del Sol, full of sun and sangria it is easy to get carried away. Feeling a soft, warm Mediterranean breeze on your tanned limbs and having nothing more taxing on your mind than whether to have the Calamares Romana or the Merlusa for lunch, you begin to think that this is the sort of life you always knew you were cut out for. Why, you wonder, do you take your job and your life so seriously? Everything is so easy here. Endless possibilities open up before you. Why not enjoy the good life whenever the fancy takes you? Like a delicious, frothy, holiday romance, you want the ecstasy to go on for ever. Spain is, after all, only a short plane-hop away, you reason. If you had a little apartment here you could be soaking it all up any weekend you liked, heck, every weekend if you liked. The difficulties associated with buying property in another country are the last thing you want to think about.

If you are lucky, your brain will kick back into action before you sign on any dotted lines. Loss of brain function is a disorder often brought on by a combination of too much sunshine and strange drinks, especially the ones sporting little umbrellas and lurid colours. Unfortunately it doesn't come into the category of infectious foreign diseases for which your doctor can give you a jab.

Another cohort of foreign property buyers comes from those who populate foreign property exhibitions held up and down the country at the weekends. Glassy eyed and obsessive in their determination to get ahead on the property ladder somewhere, anywhere, they proceed from stall to stall gathering leaflets about places from Lithuania to Liverpool with the fervour of an archaeologist interpreting the Dead Sea Scrolls. Sometimes you'd suspect that there is a killing to be made selling plots on Mars.

A HOLIDAY HOME OR A BUY-TO-LET PROPERTY?

Thankfully, most people who would like to invest abroad don't suffer from either strain of brain fever. They are often not sure, however, whether they want a holiday home or a buy-to-let apartment and are, justifiably, nervous about differences in laws, customs and traditions and how they might impact on their property purchases.

The first essential is to decide what you want. A holiday home is an entirely different proposition from a rented apartment abroad. Combining the two is difficult, if not impossible. It sounds like a good idea to buy a place, at home or abroad and let it out when you don't want to use it yourself, but the reality can be different.

Pilar, originally from Madrid and now living in Cork, had always hankered after a place in her native country. Her husband, a Cork man, heard about apartments being built in a resort near Alicante and organised a trip to investigate. They liked the area and they consider-ed it a good investment mainly because it was near a golf course. They knew that accommodation is at a premium for golfing holidays. The apartment, though small, was nicely laid out and decorated. To finance their purchase they took out a second mortgage, thereby releasing some of the equity in their home. The idea was to let it most of the time, using the rent to defray costs and to enjoy it themselves for an occasional week or two.

The practical difficulties didn't take long to assert themselves. First, they found that the times when they wanted to use the place were precisely the times when the golfers wanted it too. Then, although there are direct flights from Cork to Alicante, the full journey, including the 70-minute trip from Alicante to the resort took all day, making weekend visits impossible. The fare was a problem too, being much more than they had anticipated, despite no-frills airlines and dot-com fares. Taking their two teenage kids with them turned out to be prohibitively expensive but they were reluctant to leave them at home alone. They had bargained for running costs of €1,500 annually, roughly similar to what the selling agent had predicted. They quickly realised that when all of the ongoing expenses were taken into account they would have little change out of €3,000. Not only was the yield from letting a lot less than they had budgeted for, but also, they had grave misgivings about the local agent they had employed to look after that end of things. It may have been only a symptom of their more general disenchantment but they wondered if the apartment was occupied for much longer than they were paid for.

The whole project turned out to be an unmitigated disaster when, finally deciding they had had enough, they went back to the estate agent with a view to selling the place. Like the other agents they subsequently approached, he was far more interested in flogging the huge number of new properties then springing up all over the place than in dealing with their sale which would have netted him a much smaller fee. They finally sold it themselves over the internet to a retired British couple who wanted to join their friends who had moved there earlier. The friends had, incidentally, tipped the purchasers off that there was better value to be had in second-hand rather than new apartments.

This is not a true story, but it could be. All of the elements of it have been experienced by people I have met who have invested in Spain. If you are considering buying a holiday home abroad make sure to get your sums right. Assume worst-case scenarios in all cases and at least you won't be disappointed. When you buy abroad be prepared for every aspect of the project – from purchase, to repairs, to letting and management – to be more difficult, more expensive and to take longer than you expect.

Language is only the most obvious of the hurdles you could face. Did you know, for example that in Spain, Italy and France the costs associated with a purchase could be up to 15 per cent of the purchase price, or that in France a non-refundable 10 per cent deposit is required when a preliminary contract is signed. Legal systems differ enormously from country to country and many show far less concern for the rights of the consumer than our own does.

Do your homework by working out the answers to the following questions.

- How will you finance your purchase?
- How often will you use it?

- Is it near an airport?
- Are there direct flights to the area?
- How expensive are the fares?
- How long does it take to get there?
- Can you pay for it without too much reliance on letting?
- Have you enquired locally about the availability of tenants?
- How will you let and manage it?
- Who will clean the place and maintain it between lettings?
- Have you studied the legal system in the country of your choice, enough to know the pitfalls at least?
- Have you familiarised yourself with all of the taxes and charges you will incur, including local ones?
- If renovation or repairs are required how will you manage to get the work done? If you don't speak the language, you cannot organise anything over the phone.
- Are you familiar with the building regulations and planning requirements?
- Is it worth it? You could pay for a lot of hotel accommodation with the money you spend on a property. There are other investments, many of them with less potential for trouble, for people without large amounts of cash to spare.

Remember
Insurance rates, stamp duty, property taxes, local taxes, and water and refuse charges differ enormously from one country to another.

INVESTMENT PROPERTY

Buying investment property abroad must be subject to the usual rigorous examination with which you would approach any other business proposition. Too often in this area financial considerations get mixed up with sentiment, and common sense flies out the window. Entranced by the idea of a *pied-à-terre* in Paris, it is easy to see how the unwary can quickly become the disillusioned. Yes, I know Prague is one of the most beautiful cities in the world, and Budapest, another wonderful city, has been one of the first of the new EU states to attract foreign buyers. Call me unromantic but this is an investment we are talking about. If you want to invest in property abroad, in one of the new accession states of the EU perhaps, there may be good reasons why you should, but you will have to be prepared to do much homework in advance to find out what best suits your needs. Don't rely on sales people to set you straight. Their only interest is in making sure they sell you something. Knowing nothing about either the country you are about to invest in or the practicalities of what you are considering is no excuse for hanging on the every word of a smooth-talking sales person and soaking it all up like Holy Writ.

Your first port of call, even before you venture out to visit one of the property exhibitions, should be to your financial adviser, your bank manager, accountant or mortgage broker. A thorough assessment of your financial position should be made. Don't forget that you are dealing with fairly risky investments and the last thing you want to do is jeopardise your financial future on a whim. While the money may be easy to raise, you will be paying it back for a long time. Also, unless you are very familiar with the rental scene in the location of your choice, income is extremely difficult to predict. Tenants, I'm told are thin on the ground in parts of Eastern Europe. The possibility of unemployment, illness, divorce and the plethora of other human problems, which might arise in your life, need to be taken into account. You should have sufficient means to be able to weather these storms.

A RECONNAISSANCE MISSION

Before you take a trip to view specific properties you need to have figured out exactly what it is you want to buy. To get to this stage the exhibitions should help. Talk to the agents there and ask them all the hard questions about location, price, taxes, other expenses and the possibilities for letting. Do not go along simply to listen, but be proactive in asking for information. Decide on the price that you want to pay and stick to it rigidly. Go to your local library or to the internet and find out about any country you are considering – not just the tourist stuff, but the hard facts as well.

I once went on one of those viewing trips to Spain, which was paid for, in part, by a company hoping to sell me an apartment. Accompanied by my friend who was, like myself, mildly interested in buying a holiday home, we set off with completely open minds. From start to finish it was an extraordinary experience. From the time we landed we were shepherded from place to place by our guide and shown one apartment after another. We were never allowed out of sight for long. Luck had smiled on us, she said, as there were still a few apartments left in the more exclusive end of one development. The developer was ready to begin somewhere else and would sell the few remaining villas and apartments at 'knockdown prices' just so that he could close his books and move on. After two days of non-stop activity and a continuous sales patter about the excellence of the locality, the builder and the investment, our guide began to show signs of impatience and demand that we make up our minds about which apartment or villa we were going to take. On the previous night my friend and I had managed to go AWOL for a few hours and ended up in a local restaurant. While there, we got talking to some English people who were already living in the locality. Dire warnings about what can happen to the unwary followed. In Spain, it is not uncommon, it seems, for a developer to build on land he does not own. He can subsequently buy the site from the proceeds of the sale of the buildings. The implications for a purchaser should the said builder go bankrupt could be horrendous.

Other stories followed about foreigners buying villas off the plans only to find later that the schemes didn't even exist. Accounts of purchasers making stage payments, having over 90 per cent of the money paid and then waiting up to four years for completion of an apartment did little to reassure us. We were, they told us, luckier than the German viewers of the previous week who were brought in on buses, wined and dined by their hosts the agents, and then given contracts to sign while under the influence of the free liquor.

We woke, sadder and wiser the following morning. Under pressure to make up our minds and complete our purchase, we only wanted to get out of the place. Out of curiosity, we went along with the guide's itinerary. Nothing prepared us for what happened next. Accompanied, or rather frog-marched, into an office which we were told belonged to a lawyer, or *notario*, we were presented with a floor plan of an apartment, a picture of what the finished block would look like, a site-plan and, scariest of all, a contract, which was entirely in Spanish. When we pointed out that we couldn't understand any of it, its terms were perfunctorily explained. A pen was produced and we were advised to sign. No questions were asked about finance but it was explained that we would next be brought to a Spanish bank where we could open an account. When we refused to sign anything we were more or less dumped out. The solicitor said he was very busy and had other clients to see.

This happened about five years ago and to this day I have no explanation for the strangeness of the whole affair. Certainly the solicitor's office was the oddest I have seen. There wasn't a law book in sight, no folders or long brown envelopes, none of the musty paraphernalia usually associated with solicitors' offices. Neither was there a computer or a secretary. A single, framed certificate on the wall was the only evidence of human habitation in the entire place. My lasting impression is that we must have looked like two right eejits if both the guide and this solicitor expected us to sign that contract. Anybody with even a minimum of common sense couldn't sign so vague a document. It was also not explained for whom the solicitor was acting – us or the developer – a fundamental issue, which should have been made clear from the start.

On the positive side, many Irish people have had very good experiences with property purchases in Spain and other places. Property prices have risen sharply in the last decade in many countries and people who bought early are now very happy that they took the risk. For every negative report about investing abroad there is no doubt another view. Spain was the first place where the Irish invested in large numbers. With property prices there rising at an annual rate of 10–15 per cent over the last five years, obviously a lot of people have made money and must be quite pleased with themselves.

As the EU has expanded to include 10 Eastern European countries, bringing total membership to 25, new opportunities are opening up for Irish investors. With rents at home beginning to slow, this area may prove to be the hope for the future. At the time of writing, there is very little data on which to base a judgement. The issues involved are complex and new to us. It is essential that we expand our horizons with our eyes wide open.

SOME FUNDAMENTALS TO REMEMBER
A few fundamentals should not be forgotten.

- If you don't understand it don't sign it. This applies to contracts but equally to other documents.

- In some countries, Spain for example, mortgages are attached to the property rather than the individual. Be absolutely sure you are not taking on a large existing debt when you take on a property.
- Never allow yourself to be rushed into anything while on a fact-finding mission. Come home, back to reality and away from the sales hype before you commit yourself to anything. If it is worth considering, you can go out again to have another look.
- Have your mortgage arranged beforehand. There is no point in wasting time viewing property only to discover later that you will not qualify for a mortgage.
- Don't forget to factor in the costs associated with the purchase. They can be much higher than in Ireland.
- Take taxes very seriously. Unlike the situation in Ireland, failure to comply fully with tax law could land you in prison or lead to the seizure of your property.
- The income tax question is made easier by the existence of double-taxation agreements which are in place between Ireland and 42 other countries. These agreements apply not only to income tax but to corporation tax and capital gains tax. The effect on an Irish person, domiciled in Ireland, is that he or she pays tax to the Irish government on all income whether that income is earned in Ireland or abroad. Countries like Croatia and Bulgaria where many Irish people are currently considering investing are included in the 42, while some countries, Canada, for example, are surprisingly absent. The current list is available on the Revenue Commissioner's website, www.revenue.ie. If you wish to invest in countries not on the list all is not lost, however, as there are provisions which allow for credit relief for tax paid in another country.

INVESTING IN THE UK

For over a decade now buying in the UK has been a popular option among Irish investors. Mortgage lenders in the business of providing loans to Irish people buying in Britain have seen a 50 per cent rise in two years. In 2003 Irish buyers are believed to have invested up to €1 billion in UK property, the bulk of it going into residential units. Steep price rises have made it increasingly more difficult, however, to get a foothold in this market. Initially, London apartments were the main focus of attention but as they rose in price, they went beyond the means of many. Attention then turned to cheaper areas, the north of England in particular. Good returns have been made on capital invested in this area where prices have risen by around 20 per cent per annum.

There are companies targeting the Irish investor at the moment. Readily accessible on the internet, they also advertise widely in the property pages of the national papers. They will blind you with statistics and the gloss on their brochures. Tables of figures purport to demonstrate the great gains being made in the last few years. Without doubt some have benefited handsomely from their investments as property prices have skyrocketed in Britain. Price growth has been running at about 15 per cent per annum in the UK overall in the last few years. It must not be forgotten, however, that the fundamentals of the British housing market differ markedly from our own.

Experts have made much of the fact that the number of housing units built in Britain last year was only three times that of Ireland even though the population is 15 times greater. It is suggested that a shortage of houses will lead to ongoing, substantial price rises. To accept this is to forget that the UK has always enjoyed a more plentiful supply of housing compared to Ireland. Successive governments have undertaken major public housing initiatives since the end of the Second World War, leading to a much higher housing stock relative to demand.

In Britain the key factor seems to be location. A few years ago I watched a TV documentary showing huge areas of Manchester, which were impossible to live in, the 'sink estates' as they called them. Property prices had dropped in these areas to such an extent that houses were being abandoned. People were simply moving out and throwing away the keys. Things have certainly improved since then. Manchester is now bright, lively and buzzing, though how deep the change goes is difficult to gauge from here. Behind the gloss there are still large areas of dereliction. It is necessary to do a lot of homework to get it right in any area unfamiliar to you. Spend some time, weeks if possible, to get to know as much as you can about the area. Use this time to build local contacts with solicitors, builders, property managers and others.

As with any other investment, if you are considering buying property in Britain, make sure that you have the latest, most accurate information on which you can base sound judgements and sensible decisions. Do not forget monetary considerations. As the UK is not part of the eurozone, currency fluctuations and divergent interest rates may cause problems. With the help of your advisers factor in worst-case scenarios and see how you would cope. The usual warning given about financial products – *'past performance is no guarantee of future returns'* – is appropriate here too.

Section Three

Making the Most of What You Have

Chapter 14
Selling Your Property

There are many reasons for selling property. People move on, plans change, families grow, some get rich and others become poorer. Whatever the reason, a lot of properties change hands each year. There has been an unprecedented increase in government revenue from stamp duty in the last few years, not just because of the huge increase in prices, but because the number of transactions has also increased dramatically. Loan providers tell us that the average life of a mortgage is now below seven years, down from eight years, less than a decade ago. Traditionally, spring and early summer is the prime selling season. *'Sell in May and go away'*, the old adage of the stock exchange could equally apply to the property market. Whether the reason is the lengthening evenings, the improvement in the weather or the fact that people tend to get restless at this time of the year, nobody knows.

WHY YOU SHOULD TRUST YOUR ESTATE AGENT
When a decision to sell is made, the first port of call is usually an estate agent who will come, look the place over and give his professional opinion on what it is worth. In the past, if you were lucky, he would make one or two suggestions regarding what you might do to make the property more presentable. He would bring a few potential buyers to view and there would be an offer, maybe another offer or two, from other potential buyers. Then a bit of verbal tennis about the

price and a bit of macho shape throwing to lend a bit of colour to the proceedings would take place. After a few weeks he would tell you that the offer he had just received was probably as good as you would get and that you would be advised to take it; all very predictable stuff. Especially so, when you realised that the agent always had more buyers than properties to sell.

The estate agent's aim was to get the properties off his hands as quickly as possible so that he could spend his time actively hunting down further properties to sell. Each sale made him a fee of 1–3 per cent of the selling price. But that was then and this is now. Such a picture of your local auctioneer is to a modern estate agency practice as Rigsby, of *Rising Damp* fame, is to the modern property owner.

Today a professional, well-run agency is very efficient. It has to be. Not only that, but the larger agencies now expend considerable resources, both time and money, on research and consultations on behalf of their clients. While you might consider the fees you pay your agent to be on the high side, the costs associated with even a small agency, are enormous. The service you receive when selling your particular property is only a small fraction of the time put in by a good agent. There are brochures, or at the very least, leaflets to be designed and printed. There are telephone calls to interested parties and advertising to be organised. Not only that, but there are few jobs where more effort can be wasted. An agent may make many visits to a property before it sells. A month's work can count for nought when a seller withdraws his property from the market. Even when he thinks his job is done, almost one third of all sales fall through. All of this activity costs, and not only time and money. Is it any wonder that the burnout rate is high among auctioneers and estate agents?

Larger agencies also put a great deal of resources into market research, for which there is no immediate return. Much information on the state of the market, invaluable to government and investors is gathered by agencies that have branches nationwide. They produce highly respected reports on market trends, which, if the government commissioned them, would probably cost the taxpayer millions of euro.

A good agent will work hard at selling your property. You will know how good he is from the moment he walks in the door with a viewer. It's not what he says as much as the way he handles the job. He will have done his homework and will only show the property by appointment with you and to good prospects. Communication will be a priority and you will be kept informed about developments as they occur. When offers are made your agent will be in a position to evaluate the strength of each one and advise you accordingly. The highest offer isn't always the one most likely to work out to your best advantage as the financial strength of the purchaser must also be taken into account. The agent can often see things from a broader perspective.

Many sellers put pressure on agents to achieve higher prices than their properties warrant. The neighbour down the road gets a very high price for her place, so everybody else expects to match it, regardless of the fact that the neighbour had a garden which is twice as big as the others and a conservatory to the rear. Correct pricing is crucial to every sale. Accept your agent's advice here and in relation to offers. Sometimes owners are unaware that waiting an extra month for a relatively small increase in price may, in fact, be counter-productive. The proceeds from the sale, if invested, could yield a much greater return. Trust your agent to know when it's best to clinch a deal on an existing offer.

You don't need to be quite so trusting of your agent when it comes to presenting your property, however. It's up to you to make the most of what you have to offer. One way to do this is to try and identify your buyer, anticipate what that person's needs are and satisfy them. Ask your agent what type of person the buyer is likely to be. Will he have a family or to be a single professional? There is no way of knowing for sure who will be interested, but you should present your property with the most likely buyer in mind.

PRESENTING YOUR PROPERTY

This is often called *'staging'* or *'house doctoring'*. We live in an era where appearance is everything. Fashions in interiors have become almost as ephemeral as those in clothes. Buying a house is, for many, no longer a question of *'How many bedrooms do I need?'* or *'Does it have a downstairs loo?'* Today, a potential buyer or renter, especially if he is under 40, is more likely to want to buy into a lifestyle as to purchase or rent mere bricks and mortar.

You can have gracefully proportioned rooms, great space, a fine garden where the children can be happy and safe from dawn to dusk, but it can count for less than it should when it comes to selling or letting your house. (While 'selling' is referred to throughout, the same principles apply to letting.) If the front is adorned with stone cladding, you have carpet in your bathroom and a pair of adorable garden gnomes in your rockery, you have already knocked thousands off the value of your home. 'Naff' is a term of abuse levelled at patterned carpets, the Spanish dolls your children brought back from holidays and the net curtains which stop the neighbours watching your every move. Perhaps I am overstating the case but this is no laughing matter. A recent survey carried out for the BBC programme *The Million Pound Property Experiment* has revealed that you can do serious damage to the value of your property by putting it on the market sporting some of these features. While no similar study has been done in this country, *'aesthetic correctness'* like its close relative, *'political correctness',* is a force to be reckoned with throughout the developed world. Was it the economist John Kenneth Galbraith who said that in an affluent society people can no longer distinguish between luxuries and necessities? We also live in a society where it seems the more money we have, the less time we can spare for activities like doing up our homes. People under 40 are now, by and large, in households where both partners work. Home maintenance is the last thing they want to do when they come home after a long, working day. Places that are ready to move into are at a premium. For many younger buyers the ideal would be to personalise the space merely by hanging their own pictures and arranging the music collection.

Remember
If we are in the business of selling our property we have to do our best to give the buyer what he wants.

A QUICK FIX

Let's try to see our property as a viewer might. It is reasonable to conclude that the location is suitable since he has turned up. There isn't much we can do about where the property is anyway, but there is a lot we can do to improve its desirability. Do a thorough appraisal, inside and out, from the roadside to the back garden, upstairs and down. With notebook in hand, write down everything that strikes you as needing attention, out of place, or fit only for the dump. Take particular note of minor repairs which need to be done, such as

missing handles on doors, broken hinges, loose shelves and so on –
the sort of things you always meant to get done but never got around
to it. This is only the beginning. Now try to see how your rooms can
be greatly improved by a few small adjustments. Remember the
objective is not the convenience and comfort of the family, but to
present the house in a way that will attract someone to it. Your first
task, if you have succeeded in getting someone else to take care of the
repairs, is to clean everything in sight. Consider getting in contract
cleaners for a once-off deep clean. Expensive it may be, but necessary
if you can't face the task yourself. You might find it easier to keep the
place spruced up if you start with everything gleaming.

Think in terms of light and space. Check the level of lighting in
every room. Softer lighting is the ideal and can be achieved by clever
use of lamps and spotlights. Simply putting in higher wattage bulbs
will probably only cause glare. Uplighters can be used to make a room
look higher, while downlighters make the ceiling seem closer and can
produce wonderful shadows. Pale, neutral colours give a better sense
of space and are more restful than dark, strong ones. You could do a
lot worse than paint your entire house an off-white shade. Pick one
accent colour for each room, perhaps red, blue or black, all of which
go well with blonde wood, highlighting it in accessories like cushions
and curtains so that the whole effect will not appear bland. Use richer
tones like cherry, royal blue or aquamarine for darker woods.

All passageways should be kept clutter free as untidiness and mess
suggests carelessness. The buyer will wonder what else in the house
has been neglected. If your family has a lot of possessions – and what
family doesn't nowadays? – it might be better to get them out of the
house while you are trying to sell it. When viewing property myself I
have sometimes felt like an intruder when surrounded by the owner's
possessions. Box everything not in day-to-day use and persuade your
sister, a friend or your mother to put them in the garage or the spare
room. If that's impossible then relatively cheap, secure storage is
available in lock-up units in most cities and towns. Most houses have
too much furniture. We all accumulate items we like as we go along,
adding to what's already there and rarely dumping anything unless it's
really awful. Dump or store anything that's in the way or superfluous.

Remember, this is not forever – it's just temporary while the house
is for sale. Get your family to co-operate with you in your aim to keep
the place clean and tidy. They may object to restrictions being placed

on them but remember your objective is to sell your property as quickly as possible for the most amount of money you can get. Try to get them involved. They might all be the better for it. You can promise them a day trip to their favourite spot as a reward when the proceeds of the sale come through.

Try to create separate spaces within your home for all of the activities you engage in – dining, cooking, watching TV, reading, and so on. The buyer needs to be able to imagine his own family living in your house, doing all of the things they would normally do, but with a little more style than before.

First Impressions
Research shows that about 50 per cent of buyers make their minds up for or against a property even before they go in the front door. This is why it is important that the outside of your home looks attractive and welcoming. I have, on occasion, seen potential buyers who had arranged to view a property slow down and drive off again at speed without even stopping. First impressions do count and your house needs to have what the experts call *'kerb appeal'*. If the viewer is in a positive frame of mind when he enters the house you are already halfway there. I have also observed that, the sooner in the viewing that something is seen, the more it counts. You are wasting your time prettying up the box room if the exterior has been given the thumbs down. Concentrate on the areas that will be seen first.

Whether you have rolling acres or a half a dozen paving slabs outside your door it is worthwhile having it neat and tidy.

The following suggestions may help.

Outside
- If there are walls and gates they should be freshly painted and the gate left open to look welcoming.
- Hedges should be cut, lawns mowed and shrubs trimmed.
- Dustbins should be out of sight. Erect a screen to hide them if necessary.
- Hoses, toys, bicycles and rubbish should all be cleared away.
- Paint the front door and have it looking fresh. This makes the whole house look well cared for.
- If the front wall of the house looks shabby then it should be painted.

- A good dollop of elbow grease should be applied to the door brasses.
- Clean the porch and place a healthy-looking potted plant in it.
- Windows must be gleaming, inside and out.
- Everyone has pet hates. One of mine is crooked window blinds. Make sure all curtains, drapes and blinds are straightened and pulled so that each window looks the same from the outside.
- Do some *'instant gardening'*. A huge range of plants is available all year round in your local garden centre. Even in the dead of winter a few pansies at the front door will gladden the heart and bring cheer to the dreariest garden.

Hallways

Here, more than anywhere else, the need for space and light is most acute. A lot of hallways are dark and uninspiring. Some of the following tricks will help to brighten yours and make entering your home a pleasant experience.

- Paint it in a pale, slightly fresh colour. Gardenia is a good one. Buttery yellows, soft greens and fresh creams are good too as long as they are not too strong.
- Paint all doors leading off the hallway in the same colour.
- If the carpet has seen better days, replace it. The new one need not be expensive, just new and fresh. Economical laminate flooring can look good, though I know some people have an aversion to it.
- Make sure the lighting is effective. A strategically placed halogen or spot is a great way to light up a dark corner.
- An ugly radiator can be boxed to look better and provide a handy shelf.
- Remove all but one or two of the family photographs and put them into safe-keeping. Give the viewer a chance to imagine his own photos in situ.
- Make your stairs look smart so that the viewer wants to see what is on the next floor. If the hall is small have the same flooring in both the hall and the stairs.
- Try to ensure that your hallway smells fragrant while viewers are around. A heavy-duty air freshener will do the trick or use some scented candles or oils if you prefer. There is nothing worse than a pervasive smell of chips or last night's dinner when you go into

a house. Much has been made of the smell of baking bread and freshly brewed coffee. If you feel so inclined, go ahead, though at this stage I think that idea has become so hackneyed that most people would be amused if they came across it when viewing a house.

- Finally, the *pièce de resistance,* a large mirror will enhance any hall, making it look larger and brighter. Place it at right angles to a window for maximum effect. Make sure it is securely fitted to the wall to avoid accidents.

Kitchens and Bathrooms

After the hallway these are, without doubt, the rooms that sell most houses. Grime is the bugbear in most kitchens and bathrooms. We never mind our own grime, but other people's disgusts us. I invested in a steam cleaner about a year ago. It really is the best invention since the vacuum cleaner for tackling a heavy-duty cleaning problem. I think we are all becoming slightly wary of using too many chemicals in our homes. The steam cleaner uses only water and to great effect. Cleaning is the most important thing you can do with kitchens and bathrooms. Clean, clean and clean again. All surfaces should gleam. Again, watch those smells.

Try some of these tricks when you have finished the cleaning.

- Replace tiling if is old or nasty looking. New tiles can be put on over the existing ones if necessary. If you buy the tiles in a sale, and they always seem to be on sale somewhere, they can be very cheap. Beware, however, that sometimes the price reduction in the tiles is made up for with an increase in the price of the other essentials, adhesive and grout. You don't have to buy the whole lot in the same place. Shop around.
- Do not be tempted to paint the tiles. I have seen some disastrous results in this area. There is now on the market specially formulated tile paint. I haven't tried it, but it is expensive. Compare it with the cost of new tiling if you are tempted to try it. Another alternative is to put up light, timber, tongued and grooved panelling and paint or varnish it. It can look really well though it is not as durable as tiling.

- Repaint all walls in a fresh, not too bright colour. White or nearly white is very good in bathrooms.
- Consider the lighting in your bathroom. Downlighters give a soft, luxurious touch.
- Many kitchens and bathrooms have pine doors and panels that look shabby and dated at this stage. Paint them for a fresh, modern look.
- If the kitchen cupboards are beyond painting you could consider replacing the doors. Unless the presses are actually falling apart, this is an easy way to give them a new lease of life.
- Keep all signs of pets out of all rooms and the kitchen in particular. Though you might regard your pet as part of the family, to others the presence of dog hairs on the chairs and bowls of half-eaten pet food on the floor can be disgusting.
- Flooring is very important to the look of these rooms. Badly fitting, stained vinyl makes viewers wonder what lurks beneath. Replace the vinyl if you wish, but consider laminated flooring as a cheap alternative. It can give instant appeal.
- Disguise a battered, old kitchen table with a cloth.
- Don't forget fluffy, new towels in the bathroom, hanging nicely on a rail. In the kitchen, keep the dishcloth you have been using to mop up spills for the last week out of sight. Keep one or two new tea towels which can be put in position when necessary.
- Consider whether you really need curtains. They can look dusty and old. An alternative might be a cheap roller blind, a small-gauge Venetian bought in your local DIY store or some self-adhesive contact or spray on the glass which gives a frosted effect.

You will be amazed at the transformation that will occur in your home if you follow some of these suggestions. You will, I know, have many other ideas yourself. Once we start to see the possibilities there's no limit to our imaginations. These simple measures may not, however, be enough. Have a really critical look at your kitchen in particular. Consider the cost of a complete refit, cupboards, flooring, tiling and appliances. It may be a good investment if it gets you a much better price for the house. Ask advice from an estate agent. I would even get a second opinion on that one as it involves a lot of money.

The Rest of the House

If you have taken care of the entrance, the kitchen and the bathroom then give yourself a well-deserved break. You will be delighted to realise that there is little left to do. De-clutter the other rooms and paint them if necessary. Once again go for space and light, painting in a neutral colour once more and using one accent colour. In bedrooms this should be fairly soft.

- A few new accessories can do wonders. Cushions, rugs and lamps can be bought cheaply, as can ready-made curtains.
- Use soft-tone bulbs in all lamps. There are pink ones in the supermarkets, which will, literally, enable a potential buyer to see your home through rose tinted glasses. What more could you want?
- Make one focal point in each room, a fireplace or a coffee table, for example and arrange the rest of the furniture around it.
- Bedrooms should be tidy and beds made with crisp, clean bedlinen. In the interests of normal living a good idea might be to have a good full-sized cover for each bed which can be placed in position before each viewing commences and stowed away afterwards.
- Patterned carpets are very definitely out of fashion. They will make your house look tired and dated. Replace them with cheap, plain neutrals or, once again, consider laminate flooring.
- When everything is ready, just one last thing: ask a friend to look over the place. A fresh eye will often see something simple and obvious that you have missed.

These suggestions may, or may not, be ideal for your property. If you have a very expensive property or a very distinctive home for example, different measures might be necessary. Such properties often attract buyers who are looking for something a bit different, something unique. In that case you might be well advised to engage a specialist in interior design or an architect. Satisfy yourself in advance that the person you are considering is genuinely qualified in the field by asking about their previous work, as there are a lot of charlatans in this area. In an upmarket property, a buyer is more likely to be willing to pay over the odds for something that is impressive. The same basic rules apply to all property, however. A relatively modest outlay can repay your investment many times over.

Be aware, however, and this is something I can't help you with, that when the old place has been given a facelift you may not want to leave it after all! Don't say you haven't been warned.

WORKING WITH AN AGENT

Whenever I have had to choose an auctioneer to sell a property (which is not often because I rarely sell properties), I have had only one strategy. I looked at the for sale signs in the area and counted them. It was easy to see which company had the most. This was the firm, I reckoned who was busiest.

There are many factors that could be taken into account when choosing an agent to sell your property, but if the place is fairly standard you need the company which deals with a large volume of property. The individual you meet will probably be young, energetic, new to the scene and ambitious. Being an agent is a mentally and physically demanding job. After a while the best and the brightest begin to develop their own interests. Some go on to work with developers, others become developers themselves. Others still become more involved in the administration of their firms and concentrate on the larger, more lucrative deals. The new kid on the block is often the one who is most prepared to put in the effort to get the best possible price for an individual house or apartment.

When selling very distinctive or very expensive property, the rules are different. Here experience is what counts most. Best of all is an agent who is experienced in selling your particular type of property if it is off-standard as he is the one who will know how to mount an effective advertising campaign.

In addition to the fees you will have to pay the following expenses:

- advertising;
- erection of a sale board;
- photography; and
- VAT on fees.

An advertising budget should be worked out in advance so that you know exactly how much you will pay. Do *not* allow yourself to be talked into signing over sole selling rights to any agent. While I would recommend that you don't place your property with another agent until the first one has had a reasonable time to sell it, a sole agency gives the agent the right to be paid whether or not he does the business. Your cousin from Galway might decide that your house is just what she is looking for, or you might change your mind about selling, but the agent could still claim his fee. A more equitable arrangement would be for you to agree to cover his costs in the event of the property being sold or taken off the market.

Beware of rogues. As in every profession, there are a few rotten apples in the auctioneering trade. A dodgy character could perpetrate a number of nasty tricks. Below is a list of some of them.

- Quoting an asking price that is too high; because they know that you will shop around, they reckon that you will give them the sale in the mistaken belief that they can work some magic and get more for the property than it is worth. This trick is designed to appeal to your vanity because you, like everybody else, want to believe that your house is worth a fortune.
- Looking after their friends – a case of *'you scratch my back and I'll scratch yours'*. They fail to pass on offers from buyers other than from the said friend. Another name for this practice is bribery and corruption.
- By undervaluing a property, they make a quick sale. The property is later resold at a much higher price and the profit shared between the auctioneer and the purchaser.

Security lies in dealing only with auctioneers and agents who are members of professional bodies such as IAVI or IPAV.

Courtesy dictates that you should expect your agent to ring you and make an appointment to show the property, though this is not always possible. Each viewer should be accompanied around the property by the agent who will point out all of its good points. It is probably better if you are not there on the first visit of a potential buyer, as many people feel embarrassed when viewing a house with the owner in attendance. On a subsequent viewing the same purchaser will probably be more relaxed and might be happy to meet you. It is always reassuring to know the person you are doing business with as it makes the prospect seem less daunting.

Feedback is reassuring but many agents are busy and don't appreciate its value. If he doesn't get back ring him yourself and find out how it went. If, after about a month, there seems to be little interest from buyers and no offers, something is wrong. Call a meeting with the agent to discover what the problem is and if no satisfactory answers emerge then consider changing agents. Six weeks should be ample time for any agent to prove his worth when selling a standard property. A unique place may, of course, take longer.

DIY SALES

If you feel you could do a better job of selling your property yourself than the agent, you might think about a DIY sale. Be warned, however, that you may not save as much as you think. For a start you will face significantly higher advertising costs than an agent as he may have potential purchasers already on his books and also gets a good deal from newspapers. You will have to cover the costs of producing some sort of brochure and of posting it or e-mailing it to those who want it. If you value your time then you will waste a lot of it showing the property to people who are simply curious neighbours, fantasists and those whom you know couldn't get their act together to buy a carton of milk, let alone a house. And these are the ones who turn up! At least a third won't, but you will have to wait for them anyway. You will spend ages answering the same questions, over and over, on the phone. And then there is the security aspect. You run the risk of letting some odd character into your home. Such people are less likely to approach a business than a private individual, and agents are used to getting rid of them anyway. If you are still determined and nothing I can say will dissuade you, go ahead then, Good Luck!

Once you have found a buyer and have agreed a price, a sale closing date (be realistic here, give it about two months), then the sale can proceed in the usual way. Contact your solicitor giving him the name of the purchaser's solicitor and the agreed details. He will draw up a contract of sale which will be signed by both parties.

Chapter 15
Adding Value

CAPITAL APPRECIATION

Since the early nineties almost all property has increased about tenfold in value. People now starting out on the property ladder are sea-green with envy at those who got in early. But back then we had to contend with interest rates over four times what they are now – investing in property has never been a painless process. Experts are agreed that double-digit annual price rises will soon be a thing of the past. They *may* be right. Five years ago, however, some of the same experts were issuing warnings of the imminent collapse of the property bubble. Taking a longer term view, a rise of 5 per cent to 7 per cent is widely accepted as the average annual price increase over time. It's just that, unlike other goods, property price increases never occur in a linear fashion. If you think of property price increases as a graph it looks something like a flight of stairs, sharp rises followed by relatively flat stages. If you are anxious about the commitment you are undertaking, look back to Chapter 1 to remind yourself why buying your own home is such a good idea.

Capital appreciation can be enhanced by judicious improvements and extensions. We have all witnessed the phenomenon of a particular house or apartment achieving over the odds in price. Sometimes it's down to luck, but more often it's due to a touch of style, which can be achieved fairly easily.

REGULAR MAINTENANCE

Investing in a home you already own is often one of the best property decisions you can make. Way back in Chapter 1 we examined the reasons why buying a place on your own is worthwhile. Now we will look at ways to take care of your investment. You may find maintaining your home, year in year out, a drag, but a property that is not adequately maintained will deteriorate rapidly.

When I go abroad on holiday one of the things I like best is to look at buildings being constructed. It is interesting to see how building techniques vary in line with local customs and climatic conditions. In Norway, for example, the timber houses are wonderfully insulated against the cold. In most of Spain the relative lack of moisture allows far less consideration of water damage than it does here.

Water is the single biggest factor in maintaining your property in this country. It can cause major problems in every area of your house, so keeping it out is essential. It can be a silent killer. A small leak may go undetected for years until suddenly it becomes obvious and you find it has caused untold damage. Your roof is your first defence against water. It should be checked once a year and any loose, cracked or broken tiles should be attended to. So should any breaks or deterioration in the lead flashing in areas such as around the chimney. Have a good look from a distance, front and back, at the roof, gutters and downpipes as problems are often more apparent from a distance. Gutters should be cleaned regularly especially in the autumn when they are liable to fill up with leaves. Check the drains too from time to time to ensure that they are not blocked. Paintwork, apart from looking well, acts as a preservative, keeping dampness in the walls and exterior woodwork at bay. Yes I know all of this is very boring, but if you follow a good, annual maintenance routine you will save yourself a huge amount of time and expense in repairs at a later stage.

BUILDING ON AND BUILDING UP

In Chapter 14 we looked at ways of doing a *'quick fix'* on your property to make it attractive to a buyer or renter. I have heard many people make the comment that their home never looked as well as it did when they spruced it up for sale and that they were almost sorry to be leaving! What a pity that they didn't enjoy their home at it's best all along.

With this in mind, we can think about how someone who has no plans to move can improve their home. The aim is to add maximum value with minimum effort. Perhaps the family has expanded and grown so more living room space or an extra bedroom is required. It is important to know which of the many options available – converting the attic, building a bedroom over the garage, adding a conservatory or putting in a new kitchen – is going to add most to the value of your home. You don't, I'm sure, want to slavishly follow the market, only doing what will bring most financial gain – who wants to live in an investment! But, because we never know what the future will hold, and someday you might want to sell, it is important that at the very least you don't actually *reduce* the value of your property. Also, as the various possible improvements and additions do not confer equal benefits on all properties, you may want to consider just how much it is worth spending on a particular project.

The first step must be to set a budget for your improvements – and you have to be prepared to stick to it. Remember that the chances of completing the job within this budget, despite your best efforts, are fairly small, so it is important that your initial budget errs on the side of frugality rather than the opposite. Ask an estate agent what would be the likely maximum value for your house if the extension were done and compare this with the price of a standard house. This will give you an idea of how much you can spend. Make sure that the budget is right for the house as well as for the job to be done. There is no point, for example, in putting a very expensive kitchen into a small house. It might cost €20,000 and only add €5,000 to the value of the property.

There is no universal rule that says you will get your money back on any addition or improvement to a house. You may, however, decide to go ahead with an extension for reasons that have to do with comfort even if there is little to be gained in financial terms. The general consensus among estate agents is that stand-alone houses, where the value is less certain, increase more through add-ons and other improvements than more standard houses. Houses in estates and apartments, it seems, gain *least* from improvements.

CONVERTING THE ATTIC
Some attics are ideal for conversion. If, when you open the hatch, you can see an enormous amount of space only waiting to be put to better use than housing discarded schoolbooks and junk, then you may well

be in business. Whether or not your attic is suitable for conversion depends largely on the type of roof supports used in construction and the strength of the joists, which will take the weight of the floor underneath. You will see what I mean as soon as you look at the roof space. If there is a reasonable amount of open space between the two sides, then that looks promising. Some roofs, especially those of a more modern type are constructed using roof trusses in which a larger number of supports are used in a sort of herringbone arrangement. Though this type of roof is obviously more difficult to deal with, all is not lost. A specialist in attic conversions, and there are many of them about, will be able to redesign the roof supports, though it will, naturally, increase the cost.

In older houses there can be further problems. The beams which hold the ceiling are sometimes not strong enough to take a floor above so they must be strengthened. For all of these reasons it is essential to have your conversion properly designed. Building and planning regulations may also quite restrictive. If, however, you are determined enough to cross all of these bridges you could dramatically increase your living space. A teenager's bedroom could be an ideal use for this space. If you want to use it as a study, be sure to point this out to your architect or engineer as the weight of a large number of books might cause problems later on.

However you decide to use your attic, make sure you fit proper stairs. If you try to scrimp by putting in one of those fold-up or ladder-type stairs, you will be less likely to make good use of the space. This type of stairs is so difficult to use and feels so insecure that most people will find excuses not to go up there unless absolutely necessary.

Below are a few more practical suggestions.

- The attic can be more exposed to the elements than other parts of the house so good insulation, ventilation and heating must not be forgotten.
- Smoke alarms are even more important here than elsewhere as escape may be more difficult.
- Be sure to revise your fire escape routes, taking the new space into account just as soon as the conversion is completed.

On the design front there are few worries if you are simply putting in roof windows such as Velux or similar as they are unobtrusive on the outside. Also, planning permission will probably not be required if these windows are placed in the rear roof. Dormer windows are often preferred, however, as they can dramatically increase the amount of space and light in a room. This can create a problem, especially in smaller or terraced houses where the windows can dwarf the original building, making it far too top-heavy to be pleasing to the eye. It is essential, in most cases, to secure planning permission for dormer windows.

Once again relying on the agents, the general opinion is that a good attic conversion, fully compliant with planning, fire and building regulations can increase the value of property by two or even three times of the cost of the work.

A USEFUL EXTENSION

If carting your books up to the loft and down again is not your idea of fun, or if the project proves too costly or tricky to be viable, then you might consider an extension to the rear of the house. Once again find out the maximum value of your house before you extend and decide if it's worth it in monetary terms. Adding a room can be a great asset to the house but it must be aesthetically pleasing in order to add value. There is nothing more likely to make potential purchasers back off than a dodgy extension. This is one where either the construction or the standard of finish leaves much to be desired.

A number of factors must be taken into account before embarking on any extension.

- An extension should always blend with the style and age of the original property. It should look natural, not like something *'stuck on'* to the original building.
- The scale is important. It should not be so big that it dwarfs the house but should be in proportion to the size of the building.
- Don't forget that if it is to be of reasonable size, an extension can take up a large amount of space. This may seriously curtail your use of your garden.
- If space permits, and within the constraints already mentioned, be generous with the size. An extra half metre on one side of the extension won't cost that much more, but could make a big difference to the finished room.
- If building a ground-floor extension and the layout of the house

allows it, then at very little extra cost a foundation can be built
which is sufficient to take another floor. Then, if in future you
wish to extend your home upwards, it is a relatively simple job to
add another storey.

- In older houses avoid tearing out more than that which is
  absolutely essential. Very old houses have lime mortar rather than
  cement – in these cases cement *must* not be used as it reacts with
  the remaining lime mortar, causing rapid deterioration.
- Use reclaimed materials such as timber, slates and fireplaces in
  older buildings.
- Most rear extensions do not require planning permission unless
  they are large or 75 per cent of the garden is taken up, but check
  with the planning office in your area to be on the safe side.

What use you put your extension to is up to you. It can be a sitting
room, playroom, shower room, bedroom, office, garage or extended
kitchen. Whatever it is, it can add considerably to the value of your
house. Make sure you get the fundamentals, such as the roof,
plumbing, wiring and plastering, right and make absolutely sure it is
fully compliant with all regulations.

See Chapter 6 for more information on building.

> **Remember**
> With an old building find out about the building techniques
> and materials used originally and try to work in harmony with
> them.

ADDING A CONSERVATORY

Conservatories first came into vogue in Victorian times when great
strides in glass and wrought-iron production made them feasible as
building materials for the first time. In 1851 Prince Albert, Queen
Victoria's consort, mounted a huge exhibition in London, showcasing
the best of British manufacturing. The focal point of the exhibition
was a specially constructed building made entirely of glass called the
Crystal Palace, which must have been a marvel to behold in its day. A
problem with many conservatories today, is that they aspire to be the
Crystal Palace, though on a smaller scale. In every other area of

building things have moved on, and it is to be hoped that designers may soon advance construction design to produce contemporary conservatories that reflect the style of our modern houses. A well-designed conservatory can transform your home by greatly increasing the feeling of light and space. As with an attic conversion, it can be expected to add twice what it costs, or more, to the price of your house.

There are a number of aspects of the design of a conservatory to consider. Listed below are some suggestions.

- As with all other extensions get the scale right. Bigger isn't always better. If there is too little garden left it may have a claustrophobic feel.
- Getting the proportions right relative to the rest of the house is also essential. It must not dominate the original house, but should compliment it.
- Try to get a design that does not jar with the rest of the house. This is not easy as bespoke conservatories are horrendously expensive, but unless you live in Georgian or Edwardian splendour try to keep it simple.
- Brickwork or plaster which blends with the house help prevent the conservatory from having a *'stuck on'* look.
- Internally, one of the most important features to get right is the link between the conservatory and the main house. If there is good access and a flow from one to the other, your conservatory will be well used and enjoyed. Avoid having access to the conservatory through one small door only, as the tendency is to close this door and forget about what's beyond it. A much better arrangement is to have both the kitchen and the living room, if they are side by side, opening into the new area. This will enable people to wander from one space to the other, making the conservatory an integral part of the house.
- Do not, if at all possible, place the door to the garden directly opposite the back door of the house as this creates a corridor effect, thus limiting the use of space.

You are unlikely to need planning permission for a conservatory, but a call to the planning office is advised. Do not be tempted to build something cheap from softwood. This is false economy as it will look terrible and last only a few years. Finally, give some thought to how your conservatory will be heated. A simple extension to your existing system may be all that's required, but underfloor heating works very well, keeping the place cosy in the coldest of weather.

THINGS WHICH ADD MOST VALUE
Having converted the attic and added an extension and/or a conservatory there are a number of further improvements which will add additional value to your home.

- *Install central heating.* An efficient heating system is an essential. If your home doesn't have any central heating or if your system is old, renewing it should add more to the value than it costs. While you are at it, check for draughts and seal around any ill-fitting doors and windows.
- *Improve the kitchen.* A well-groomed kitchen is usually one of the major selling points in a property. A complete replacement should be preceded by a look at the shape of the room and the position of the appliances to see if the design minimises the walk from one area to another when working. If a complete replacement is not required or is deemed too expensive, then consider changing the doors and the worktop to give a fresh new look. Replace the central pendant with a few halogen lights. These give an ideal light for a kitchen. Lights under the upper units are very useful when cooking and are inexpensive to install.
- *Improve the bathroom.* If you don't have a power shower consider installing one. For some reason people now have an aversion to some sanitary ware colours such as avocado and chocolate brown. Such an aversion is usually an indication that something is about to come back into fashion. For now, however, white seems to be the only acceptable colour. A basic white suite won't set you back too much, but unless you intend to replace the tiles make sure it will fit in exactly the same spot on the original. A touch of luxury can be added by merely changing the fittings to newer, better designed versions. Some lovely ones are widely available now. Today carpet is even more unacceptable in bathrooms than a coloured suite. Vinyl flooring will do at a pinch, but ceramic tiles on the floor are ideal.
- *Restore the character of your house.* Many older buildings have

been subjected to much abuse in their time. If you are lucky enough to have a period house you can increase its value by undoing some earlier 'improvements' and getting back to basics. Go to the library and study building techniques and materials to know what the original was like. Remove the following if they are present anywhere in your home: woodchip wallpaper, flush doors, stone or pine cladding on walls, polystyrene ceiling tiles, fake beams and modern fireplaces. Many of these features have their uses but have no place in a restoration project where the aim is to make the building as close as possible to the original. Pay particular attention to the windows. Replicas of original timber windows can be made by good joiners. Don't worry about imperfections in the plaster. An old house will be forgiven for looking its age. It will, at least, look authentic.

- *Replace your windows.* New windows will not only make your home look smarter, but will greatly increase your level of comfort. This is especially true if they are replacing old ill-fitting ones. New building regulations mean that the standard of new windows is now very high. PVC is very popular, as it is maintenance-free and efficient. I think people are, however, beginning to get tired of ubiquitous white plastic. As with other improvements, work in sympathy with the style of the building as far as possible.

- *Tidy the garden.* Keep it well maintained, the hedges and shrubs trimmed, the grass cut. It is worth getting your garden properly designed once. You may not do a complete landscaping job immediately but you will then have a plan towards which you can work. This may actually save you money on bad choices of plants, which later have to be pulled up. A well-designed patio or deck will give additional living space and greatly enhance the appearance of your garden.

- *Be a legal eagle.* If you have a large garden which is not in use you could try to get planning permission on part of it for either another house or for a granny flat. If you succeed you will then have a very valuable asset. You can then sell the plot or build on it yourself.

- *Buy out the ground rent on your property.* When it comes to selling, a freehold property is a more attractive buy than one with a lease where ground rent must be paid. Buy some adjoining land if you can. Whoever said that land was the best investment as they were not making any more of it was right. A larger garden is a great asset as it adds potential for attractive landscaping, increased living space, more parking or for building.

THINGS YOU SHOULD NEVER DO

- Build an extension that is poorly constructed or badly finished.
- Construct an extension without planning permission.
- Add an extension that occupies the entire garden.
- Add stone cladding.
- Concrete over the front garden, unless it's to provide necessary parking space, in which case you will need planning permission.
- Reorganise your space so that you have a smaller number of bedrooms.
- Install PVC windows in a period building.
- Remove period features such as fireplaces and picture rails.

Remember
The higher the value of the property, the more important are aesthetic values.

Chapter 16
And Finally...

SOME CONCLUSIONS

In my 20 plus years involvement in the property business I have seen many changes, some good, some disastrous. Often it feels as if the most recent developments are only just beginning to be understood and acted upon when yet another adjustment reverses all our newly held beliefs and strategies. But that's life. Some things never change, however, and we all pick up some tricks of the trade and a modicum of common sense along the way, often perhaps in spite of ourselves. I offer here a few fundamentals I have learned.

General

- Be organised, write everything down and keep all of these bits of paper. This will save you many headaches later. Better still, get a notebook.
- Confirm all agreements in writing and have others do the same. You think you will remember what was decided, but you won't.
- Don't become angry with others no matter how much you are provoked. It will interfere with your judgement and your actions.
- Sort out your priorities and do the most urgent things first. This usually means doing what it takes to bring in the cash which will keep you solvent.
- Watch your use of time. It is easy to be busy 24 hours a day, being productive is another matter.

- Use your money wisely, save, invest and diversify. Don't put all your eggs in one basket.
- Don't let others walk all over you.
- Don't overextend yourself financially. Nothing is worth sleepless nights.
- Learn to recognise when it's time to cut and run, when a deal isn't working out.

For Landlords
- Treat your tenants fairly and honestly. If you do they will send you others who are already well-disposed towards you.
- Learn to listen sympathetically when your tenant has a problem. If he feels he is being heard the problem is halfway to being solved.
- Don't try to get the last penny in rent. It creates resentment.
- Develop your talents along with your property portfolio. Use the opportunities presented for personal growth.
- Don't take it all too seriously. Once you are secure in your own home that's the most important thing. After that it's only money.
- Be proud of what you do and enjoy it.

For First-Time Buyers
- Don't give up. whatever your problems choose to see them as challenges.
- Explore every possibility. I have tried to provide you with some solutions to your difficulties. There are many others I haven't thought of – but you will.
- Don't put yourself under undue strain by taking on more than you can manage. You can seriously damage your health and your relationships by piling on more stress than you can deal with.
- Finally, and most importantly, don't become confused between a happy home and a purchased one. Harmony, peace and contentment are by no means by-products of home ownership. It really is better to live happily in a hovel than miserably in a mansion!

Useful Addresses and Websites

WEBSITES

www.myhome.ie

www.revenue.ie

www.daft.ie

www.nicemove.ie

www.realestate.ie

www.let.ie

www.askaboutmoney.com

www.ascotfirst.com

www.homebuyhomesell.ie

www.threshold.ie

ADDRESSES

Irish Property Owners Association
Ormond Court, 11 Lower Ormond Quay, Dublin 1

Irish Auctioneers and Valuers Institute
38 Merrion Square, Dublin 2

Private Residential Tenancies Board
Canal House, Canal Road, Dublin 6

Department of Environment & Local Government
Custom House, Dublin 1

Revenue Commissioners Information Service
Telephone: (01) 8780100

Appendix 1

Stamp Duty Rates for Residential Property

Note: First-time buyers who are owner-occupiers are exempt from stamp duty for new properties which have a Floor Area Certificate and are under €190,500 in value, provided the property is occupied as their main residence for not less than five years. A reduced rate applies to properties above €190,500 and below €381,000.

Price	First-Time Buyers	Others
	%	%
Up to €127,000	Nil	Nil
€127,001–€190,500	Nil	3
€190,501–€254,000	3	4
€254,001–€317,500	3.75	5
€317,501–€381,000	4.5	6
€381,001–€635,000	7.5	7.5
€635,001 upwards	9	9

In the 2004 budget, the Minister for Finance announced a reduction in the rates of stamp duty payable by first-time buyers of second-hand homes. Such properties valued at €317,500 or less will now be exempt. Reduced rates will apply to properties valued above this threshold. No charges have been made in rates for first-time buyers of new properties.

Appendix 2

Summary of Tax Incentive Schemes and Cut-Off Dates

Cut-off dates may change as they have in past budgets. When these properties are sold any unused portion of the tax relief may be transferred to the new owner.

Scheme	Date
Urban Renewal	31/12/2004
Town Renewal	31/12/2004
Rural Renewal	31/12/2004
Living Over the Shop	31/12/2004
Section 50 (Student Accommodation)	31/12/2004
Park and Ride	31/12/2004
Multi-Storey Car Parks	31/12/2004
Third-Level Education Buildings	31/12/2004
Nursing Homes and Homes for the Elderly	25/03/2007
Private Hospitals and Sports Injury Clinics	n/a
Refurbishment of Relief on Rental Accommodation	n/a

In the 2004 budget, the Minister for Finance announced a review of the above schemes.

Index